Beaten Paths & Back Roads

California Stories in the Land of the Palm & the Pine

By Steve Newvine

Also by Steve Newvine

The California Series

9 from 99, Experiences from California Highway 99
California Back Roads
Can Do Californians

All books are available at Lulu.com/Steve Newvine
Selected titles available at Amazon, Barnes and Noble.com, and Bookshop.com
Selected titles available for in-person purchase at Merced Courthouse Museum Gift Shop

Copyright 2024 by Steve Newvine
ISBN: 978-1-312-18649-1
Neither this book, nor any portion of it may be reproduced in print, electronically, digitally, or by any other means without the express written consent of the author.

Beaten Paths & Back Roads

California Stories in the Land of the Palm & the Pine

By Steve Newvine

Table of contents

<u>The Mountains</u>   9

Yosemite By Car, Bicycle, Paintbrush, or Camera Lens
The Wild Fire Threat-Look for the Helpers

<u>The Coast</u>   28

Pacifica
Monterey
Pizmo Beach

<u>The Palm, the Pine and Other Important Trees</u>   35

Palm and Pine Signs
The Legacy Tree In Visalia
Calaveras Big Tree Park and Gold Country

<u>The San Joaquin Sound</u>   49

Buckaroo Reunion
Bob Hope Theatre
The Night Kenny Rogers Came to Town

<u>Building Greatness</u>   61
Cupola
Roundabouts
Rebuilding a Historic Showplace

<u>Giving People</u>   73
Kettle Stories
Fireworks
Planada
Flood Relief
Summer Program
Sad Times

A Bite to Eat   93

Wool Growers
Branding Iron
Girl Scout Cookies
Hilmar Cheese

Car, Kites, and Planes   107

Cars and Coffee
Modesto Car Museum
Kites
Electric Planes at Fresno's Chandler Airport

Agriculture   123
Nuts
Harvest Time
Bees
Inflation Pest
Ag Expo

Celebrating Community   139
Knights
Century Cities
Medic Alert
Police Escort
Underpass Art

Golf Course Aficionado   159

Hole In One
He's Seen a Lot of Back Roads
Golf Buddie Dennis

Memory Movers   169
1973

Dedication

Dedicated to the storytellers of California. For the historians, columnists, authors, podcasters, webmasters, photographers, reporters, musicians and others who have shared the compelling stories of this special state of California

Read Steve Newvine's *Our Community Story* column twice monthly column on MercedCountyEvents.com

Follow Steve's columns and stories at *Can-Do Californians* on Facebook

Introduction

You have started a journey across and up and down an amazing part of the United States. Most of what you are about to read can be found along the beaten paths and back roads of California.

With ten years working in the tourism promotion industry, and nearly fifteen years travelling the state for work-related business meetings, I have acquired an interest in seeing things we might take for granted.

In 2017, the book *California Back Roads* brought some of these places to the attention of readers. This new edition is just an extension of that earlier work with different locales, new stories, and more people telling their fascinating stories.

It has been a labor of love compiling these stories. Many of the stories have their beginnings as columns from the *Our Community Story* section of the website *MercedCountyEvents.com* . In every case, the original column has been updated with new information. In addition, there are about a dozen new stories.

The theme is pretty much as simple as the old adage my mother would utter when I was a child. When my siblings and I would complain about long Sunday afternoon rides in the family Pontiac, she would retort "You get to see a whole new world when travelling the back roads."

Whether it is the water tower seen at the beginning of the television show *Petticoat Junction*, the public golf course where the greatest water hazard is the Pacific Ocean, or the cultural influences that created the Central Valley's unique musical genre, it is all right here.

So slow down the pace, relax with a favorite beverage, and come along with me as we further explore the land of the coast, the mountains, the palm and the pine.

Steve Newvine
November 2023

The Mountains

Yosemite by car, foot, paintbrush, camera lens or other means

The iconic Half Dome at Yosemite National Park.
Photo: Steve Newvine

Yosemite National Park is one of the most spectacular sites anyone will ever see in the United States. It remains California's most visited recreation venue.

What may be the most unique feature of the Park is that all of it is on California back roads. There's no interstate exit with a five-mile connector road to take you to the park entrance. While many of the roads leading to the park have been expanded and improved over the years, Yosemite is still a place you can only get to by taking the back roads.

By Car

I first saw Yosemite from the back seat of a convertible with the top down on a cold February morning. My hosts had an old Chrysler LeBaron convertible they hung onto well past its prime just for that purpose. They believed this natural wonder was best seen from this car, and they were probably right.

With a one-hundred, eighty degree vantage point, I took in the majesty of the mountains, the splendor of the meadows, and the spectacle of the skyline. Then we got out of the car.

Depending on the distance between where the car is parked, and where the particular viewing site is located, seeing Yosemite as a walker is a great way to take in much of what the park has to offer. Visitors can walk to the base of the Bridal Veil Falls, to the base of El Capitan or even the base of Half Moon.

Hikers, especially those who have prepared well for the rigors of elevated trail navigation, can make their way along trails that veer off from the valley floor.

The biggest change to Yosemite in the past fifteen years since I made that first visit by car is the increase in the number of vehicles now entering the Park. The National Park Service would prefer fewer cars and frequently suggest bus tours as the best way to see as much as possible.

Still, we are a people who prefer the privacy of our cars. While road improvements have tried to keep pace with increased interest, the alternatives are worth considering especially in the summer season.

By Foot

Brennen Thompson about to scale Half Dome at Yosemite National Park. Photo: ValleyTough.com

What would you say if you hiked eleven mountains throughout California, and then stared at the bottom of the awe-inspiring Half Dome at Yosemite National Park.

If you were this former upstate New York transplant to California, there is just one sentence: "It's going to be long day!"

In 2020, Brennen Thompson and his climbing partner Garrett Wright began climbing mountains. Every month, the pair made their way through a series of climbs throughout California.

Starting with Sandstone Peak in southern California, they set their sights on a new mountain each month. Over the course of twelve months, they made it to Mount Wilson, San Gabriel Peak, and Mount Whitney among others.

Half-Dome at Yosemite was number twelve.

The pair wrapped up their year-plus adventure with a climb up Mount Kilimanjaro in Tanzania in the summer of 2021. Each climb w**as** done with purpose. They raised money to benefit charities in Brennen's hometown in upstate New York.

The Yosemite climb began with a 4:00 AM wake up, a breakfast of pre-cooked oatmeal with fruit, and the trip to the trailhead.

"I was surrounded by massive shadows like El Capitan and, of course, Half Dome," he said.

Midway up the cables of Half-Dome, Brennen's awareness of the gift of life was heightened. "After encountering trees the size of skyscrapers, waterfalls that couldn't be imagined, and views that take your breath away, I was a little more thankful to be alive than normal," Brennan said.

Peanut butter sandwiches, nuts, and granola kept the pair nourished during the adventure. After five hours, they made it to the top. Brennen took it all in.

"Climbing the sub-dome cables was one of the dumbest things I've ever done," he thought to himself. "Can't wait to see what they're like on the way down."

Thinking initially they would take in a few moments with the solace of nature before heading down, they met another climber who had done the Mount Kilimanjaro climb. As the pair planned on travelling to Mount Kilimanjaro for their final leg of their year-long adventure, they struck up an impromptu friendship with their fellow climber. They used the opportunity to pick his brain on strategy for the ultimate climb.

"We stayed up there longer than normal, probably an hour," Brennan said. "By then, it was time to head back down Half Dome."

It took four hours to make it back to the valley floor using the same route. "Going down the sub-dome was actually harder than going up!" Brennan explained. "Baby steps, and don't look to the left or right."

This was Brennen's first time in Yosemite. "I was overwhelmed with the beauty and couldn't have been more pleased with the hike."

As spectacular as Yosemite was, and as ambitious as the total package of twelve hikes proved to be, the real challenge would be coming up in another month on the other side of the world.

The pair headed to Tanzania, Africa later that summer and completed the promise to scale twelve major California venues plus the iconic Mount Kilimanjaro all within a year.

This pair of Californians promised to make an impact. They delivered on that promise. They raised several thousand dollars for the hometown charities, and checked off a future bucket list item. They did all of this within the first year of arriving in California.

By Bicycle

He was more than just an ordinary bicyclist. Francois Hennebert traveled from France to make the trek from Mexico to Canada. Here he is at Yosemite's Sonora Pass. Photo: [http://velo.hennebert.fr/][0]

Brennan's exploration of Yosemite was a long and satisfying journey. The same can be said of an international visitor to California. This visitor from France saw Yosemite from the vantage point of his bicycle.

When Francois Hennebert brought his broken bicycle to a Merced bike shop for repair one-day in 2018, no one knew what kind of impression he would have of the area.

Francois crossed into Merced County as part of a twenty-five hundred-mile bike trip from Mexico to Canada.

At the time, he was continuing his annual bike rides to countries all over the globe. Every year, he would spend several months traveling around the world. He took a plane to Mexico and saw three countries on his incredible bicycle trip.

Shortly upon his return to his native France, Francois posted photographs and his impressions of Yosemite, California, and the City of Merced where he was taken by a generous tow truck driver when his bike broke down in adjacent Mariposa County. Francois effectively hitched a ride in front of another visitor's station wagon that was being brought into the city for repair. The driver dropped Francois and his broken bicycle off at an area bike shop.

He had been on bike trips to China, South America, and New Zealand to name a few places. He had a website that detailed his adventures.

Prior to his unplanned visit to Merced, Francois had just completed the leg of his journey that took him to the Sonora Pass in Yosemite. Bicycling enthusiasts say the Sonora Pass is one of the most difficult biking trips a cyclist can take.

His unscheduled stop in the Central Valley opened his eyes to another side of California. In the valley, he was helped by a stranger who just happened to have a tow truck heading to Merced. While in the city, he got his bike repaired and met more friendly faces. He was overwhelmed by the team at the local bike shop who got his bicycle back in sound working condition. He expressed gratitude with the words from his website: celui va rester dans ma mémoire .

Translation: that will stay in my memory.

By Paint Brush

This covered bridge painting by Vivian Knepel was loaned to the Merced County Courthouse Museum for the Originals of Yosemite exhibition. Ms Knepel was well-known for paintings of a variety of scenes from Yosemite.

Scenes of the iconic stops within Yosemite have been painted by local artists since the early days of the Park's existence

One such artist is Vivian Knepel who has painted dozens of scenes from Yosemite over the years.

In 1980, she captured a covered bridge to her canvas. That painting was shown to the public in a program organized by the Merced Courthouse Museum in 2019.

She found most of her subjects along the back roads of Yosemite and surrounding areas. She had the generous heart to permit museums such as the Merced County Courthouse Museum, to borrow her work for special shows.

The Merced show was called *The Originals of Yosemite.* The show ran for a few months in 2019.

"My mother lived in North Fork in Madera County, having moved there from southern California back in the early 1960s." Vivian's daughter Durell Ewing told me. "Whenever she had guests visiting, it was natural for her to take them into Yosemite."

Vivian passed in 2023, but the paintings continue to keep her legacy alive. She sold many over the decades, and family members have many as part of their personal collections.

"This was her advocation," Durell said. "She did all the iconic sites, but really enjoyed the back country of Yosemite. Places where very few people would ever see."

Vivian lived to be one-hundred and four years old. She passed just two months after marking that birthday. Her paintings are in the homes of dozens of friends and relatives. Her interpretations of Yosemite remain with us for generations to come.

It's a legacy on canvas from a remarkable artist.

By Camera Lens

Photography from Roger Wynan and Jay Sousa in a 2019 exhibit at Merced College in California.

While it may be a subjective debate, Yosemite is one of the world's most photographed places.

Thousands of articles have been written about the best places to shoot photos in the Park. With cameras now in our phones, it seems as though everyone becomes a landscape photographer upon entering Yosemite.

There are professional photographers who have shared their lens' view of this jewel of nature.

Two of these professionals are Central Valley photographers Jay Sousa and Roger Wyan. Both have documented the Park for several years through their cameras.

One of the photographs from the One River- Two Perspectives exhibit in that was shown at the Merced College Art Gallery in 2020.

The pair has worked together in their separate photography businesses for many years. A few years ago, they presented an exhibit called *One River- Two Perspectives* that was shown at the Merced College Art Gallery.

Combining their efforts came naturally to them.

"My contribution features some of my favorite photographs from the Merced River and Yosemite," Jay told me during a radio public affairs program. "The region is beautiful for a photographer."

Roger is always looking for a new way to interpret Yosemite through his camera. His Facebook page is filled with images from his recreational hikes into nature. "We had an awe-inspiring hike up to the Mariposa Grove of the Giant Sequoias in Yosemite," he recently shared as he posted images from the Tunnel Tree, Grizzly Giant and the Bachelor and Three Graces.

The Tunnel Tree in the Mariposa Grove at Yosemite as seen through the lens of Merced photographer Roger Wyan. Photo: © Roger J. Wyan, All Rights Reserved

Roger's work takes him to the extremes in terms of California weather. While his photography business is headquartered in the City of Merced, his work space is the entire state.

His recent photos from Mariposa County were taken in the winter. He had to brave the elements to get the perfect shots, but all of it paid off.

"A humbling experience," he described. "Worth any discomfort from the approximate seven mile round trip hike on the snowy trail."

Photographers, the professionals as well as the casual image seekers, will endure some discomfort to get just the right photograph.

By Other Means

Highway 49 between Don Pedro Lake and Coulterville. It is a curvy two-lane road that some use as a shortcut to Yosemite. Officials say if you take it, exercise caution. Photo: Steve Newvine

Following a talk I gave to a local social club about places I've seen in California, some people from my audience approached me with their individual stories about visiting the Yosemite National Park.

One told me he has been going to Yosemite every year since he was three year's old. He added that he recently celebrated his eighty-second birthday. I remarked how I have been in the park on about a half-dozen occasions and decided to stop going because of the heavy traffic I experienced on a trip there one summer.

"Go in the fall," was his advice to me. "Travel there after the summer's end, and before the snow falls. That's the best time."

Another person shared with me the story about the time he and three friends went snowshoeing in Yosemite.

"It was only my fourth time ever being on snowshoes," the man remembered. "We hiked a trail that took us to the other side of Half Dome."

That particular hike could have been tragic as the four men reached the top toward the end of the afternoon. They started to hike back down, when the sun set. "Thankfully for us there was a full moon that night," he said. "That gave us enough light to see where we were going."

With nightfall, January temperatures began to fall and that meant the light and fluffy snow they skied on going up the peak had now turned to ice. "It was a real challenge navigating that frozen snow," he told me. "Especially for me as I was a relatively new cross country skier."

As with so many other aspects of life in California, a healthy respect for nature is a good thing to have. The smart strategy begins with knowing what might go wrong, and to have a plan to deal with that worse case scenario.

Whether it was by car, or bicycle, or even from the vantage point of an art exhibit or museum display, Yosemite National Park is the pot of gold at the end of a California back road rainbow.

Wildfire Threat- Look to the Helpers

The Oak Fire Back Office- Cal Fire's Incident Command Post in Merced, CA. Teams from the Oak Fire near Yosemite take part in a daily incident update at the command post.
Photo: Steve Newvine

It was *Misterogers* who at times would tell his public television audiences that when times turn turbulent, look for the helpers.

Anyone travelling to the mountain areas of California in the summer months may very well face the prospect of wildfires.

Once a wildfire is reported, all available resources from the state fire department known as Cal-Fire kick into action. Usually, an incident command post is set up near the fire. That was the case in Merced, California in August of 2022.

Some refer to it as the nerve center of wildfire management in California.

While the public got around the clock images and information about the Mariposa County California wildfire (named by Cal-Fire as the Oak Fire), information that helped firefighters battle the blaze was being disseminated from some fifty miles away in adjacent Merced County.

The Merced County Fairgrounds was transformed to the operational nerve center for the more than three-thousand fire fighters and support workers charged with putting out the Oak Fire.

"Ordinarily, a fire in the Mariposa County region would have an incident command post set up at the Mariposa Fairgrounds," said Cal-Fire Public Information Officer Natasha Fouts. "But the fire required more so we needed larger space."

The command post is important to be sure everyone is getting the most accurate information at the same time. During the fire-fighting campaign, a daily meeting was held at seven in the morning.

The briefing is set up like an all-hands staff meeting at a corporation. There was an agenda that included incident commanders reporting on progress, a weather forecast for the day, updates from outside agencies such as California Highway Patrol, operational changes from fire management and even a clarification on filling out expense vouchers by the finance department. After the briefing, some individual teams had smaller update sessions with their personnel.

It appeared well-organized and efficient. About twenty individual reports were made within the span of about forty minutes. Time is important to everyone. The firefighters get the information they need, and then they headed out to the scene.

Like many emergency agencies of this magnitude, Cal-Fire uses a concept known as Incident Command System (ICS). The system is an all-risk incident management concept that allows participants a structure to match the complexities of an incident like a wildfire.

The success of a firefighting effort can sometimes be threatened by jurisdictional boundaries. The ICS takes that threat into account with a standardized, on-the-scene management structure.

"The System would allow someone like me or one of my colleagues to step into any emergency situation anywhere and basically pick up the work immediately," Natasha Fouts says.

The daily incident update meeting prepares the teams for their shift up into the region where the Oak Fire is destroying forests, threatening homes and putting thousands of residents in danger. Near the end of the July 2020 fire, more than nineteen-thousand acres were burned, making this the biggest wildfire in California to that point in that year.

Sitting in on one of the daily briefings can help drive home the complicated nature of a wildfire. Leaders from the various aspects of the effort are brought up before the group for short updates. Firefighters get updates on the weather ("lower humidity in the coming days will make our jobs tougher"), safety ("remember, you represent all of us when you're traveling to the scene, watch your speeds"), and even a pep talk from one of the partners in fighting the blaze.

"Everyone in this room has chased this fire real well," one of the speakers at the morning briefing told the group. "We need everyone now to keep up the effort."

An incident report packet is made available to anyone coming into the meeting. The report contains over forty pages of information the teams can scan, make notes on, and take with them as they leave.

There is a lot happening when a wildfire breaks out in California. Fighting the spread is the top priority. But while that is going on, other agencies are preparing such things as emergency shelter for displaced residents, access for medical attention and traffic management near the area of greatest impact.

Following the incident report briefings, individual groups frequently hold short meetings specific to that group's particular role in fighting a given wildfire. Photo: Steve Newvine

Throughout the day, updates on all that is happening surrounding the fire is coordinated through the information center set up in the parking lot at the entrance to the fairgrounds. Inside, public information workers gather what's coming in, and turns it around so that everyone is getting the news in real time.

In the early days of this particular fire, an expected end date was set for the end of July. However, as the week of July 24th progressed, that date was removed from update reports. That's likely an indication as to the unpredictable nature of this particular California wildfire.

The command post comes down when it is determined there is no longer a need for this level of coordination.

As one of the speakers from the National Forest Service told the group at an earlier daily briefing, "It's absolutely remarkable, thank you very much. But the next few days are going to be clutch."

Those final days of fighting the Oak Fire in 2022 were clutch for the first responders. As *Misterogers* suggested, looking for the helpers can be comforting. That was the case then, and when something this bad happens again, once again we can look for the helpers.

The Chow Line. Firefighters working the Oak Fire in the summer of 2022 file in for breakfast the mobile kitchen set up at the Merced Fairgrounds. Photo: Steve Newvine

Author note. You can hear Steve discuss the Cal-Fire Incident Command Post in great detail by entering the words "Steve Newvine Oak Fire" in the search feature on YouTube. You will find an interview he did for KYOS radio from August 2022.

An instructor works with artists painting the cliffs at Pacifica south of San Francisco. Photo: Steve Newvine

The Pacific Ocean waves pound the rocks at the coast in Pacifica. Photo: Steve Newvine

The Coast

840 Miles of Breathtaking Views

There's more than eight-hundred miles of Pacific Ocean coastline in California. I'm been fortunate to have spent time at five locations along this span.

My first view of the Pacific was from a car crossing the Golden Gate Bridge into San Francisco. I had only been in the state a few weeks when a good friend decided to take me on a poor man's tour of the state.

That day included lunch at a Sausalito restaurant, a drive to a residential neighborhood where we thought exteriors from the Robin Williams movie *Mrs. Doubtfire* were filmed, and a drive-by the Transamerica building. All of it was exciting, although too brief to appreciate the beauty of the ocean and the then thrilling prospects of the city by the Bay.

In subsequent visits for work and pleasure, I had the opportunity to visit Alcatraz on a work-related volunteer project, see Major League Baseball games for both the Giants and the A's, go on a scavenger hunt at the Oakland Zoo, and stay at the Fairmount Hotel where Tony Bennett first sang his signature song *I Left My Heart in San Francisco*.

The Bay Area of California opened up so many opportunities for me in the thirteen years I worked for a company whose home base was in San Francisco. For most of that period of time, work required me to travel there at least once a month. Each time, I tried to take in something to remember the Bay.

Monterey

South of the Bay Area, the Monterey area brings back a lot of fond memories on a number of levels.

For about ten years, I would attend an annual conference held at a hotel in Monterey Bay. The local volunteer board would ask a few members to attend the conference every year. I accepted the invitation every year, attended the conference, and used whatever downtime I had to explore the area.

In the process, life long memories of ocean breezes, clean air, and a slower pace did the heart and the soul well.

The view from one of the tees at Pacific Grove Municipal Golf Links in Pacific Grove, California. Photo: Steve Newvine

The public beaches speak for themselves with the din of ocean waves washing up on shore. There is something ephemeral about the nightly sunsets as I take in the limited time I have before the sun disappears from view.

Nearby in the pier region of Monterey, Cannery Row captures some of the imagery from John Steinbeck's novels. I lost myself for what must have been the better part of an afternoon browsing in an antique store in Cannery Row. Surely other visitors to this or other stores in that neighborhood have done the same.

The Monterey Peninsula may be best-known for the *Seventeen Mile Drive,* the roadway that circles this patch of California. Pebble Beach tops the list of about a half-dozen world-renown courses on the Peninsula. While I have been on the grounds of Pebble Beach, I haven't had the pleasure of playing a round on this iconic course.

However, I have played the one course many of the locals play. Pacific Grove Municipal Golf Links is unique for a number of reasons. The front nine holes are in a residential section of the City of Pacific Grove. The back nine holes are along the coastline of the ocean. The front nine plays very much like a public course with the added benefit of deer near many of the greens. You'll see deer on the back nine as well, but the ocean view is the attraction here.

Throughout the back nine, here are areas of plant life that are marked with signs asking that golfers not tread into the vegetation due to the protective status. A lost golf ball in these areas remains lost.

The price is also a distinction. Green fees at Pebble Beach top over six-hundred dollars before cart and caddie fees. Green fees at Pacific Grove run in the fifty-dollar range with some breaks for twilight and junior players. Pacific Grove is the poor man's Pebble Beach.

While not speaking for all golfers, my view of golf courses centers on how I feel about being on the landscape. The views are important, but the people I meet, their stories from their experiences, the unique weather features such as ocean breezes or even an unexpected rain shower, are among the characteristics of a California coast golf outing.

I played Pacific Grove annually for about a decade. Most of those outings are just as vivid to me now as they were when I was playing the course.

Pismo Beach

A morning run along the beach at Pismo Beach. Photo: Vaune Newvine

About an hour north of Los Angeles, Pismo Beach is churning out California Dreamin' memories.

The beach town holds a personal distinction of being the second venue where I experienced the Pacific Ocean.

My wife and I were in the area returning from a trip to Solvang in the Santa Ynez Valley. We got off the highway 101 freeway and made our way to highway 1, better known as the Pacific Coast Highway.

For background, you need to know that the Pacific Coast Highway runs north and south along most of the California coastline. It shares the name with portions of other highways and is known as State Route One.

We were not sure where the beach entrance was, but we saw a cluster of cars at a public park. We decided to park there, ask around, and see what would happen.

We found ourselves in The Pismo Beach Monarch Butterfly Grove. Thousands of Monarch Butterflies flock to Pismo State Beach as it is considered a place that's essential to successful migration.

From late October to February, the butterflies cluster to the Eucalyptus trees throughout the Grove. We were overwhelmed by the large number of Monarchs that seemed to cover every inch of the Eucalyptus trees.

According to the *ExperiencePismoBeach.com* website, there were an estimated twenty-two thousand Monarchs in the Grove during the Spring 2022 count. Yes, they actually do something that looks like a count of the number of butterflies. Tracking the numbers can provide information on how the species is doing from year to year.

Grade school students from several districts made their way to the Grove to take in this true marvel of nature. We just happened to stumble onto it.

Thank goodness for serendipity.

We eventually found the beach and enjoyed a great day in the southern California sun. I have been fortunate to have returned to Pismo Beach several times in the nearly two decades I have lived in California.

As breathtaking as the beach view of the ocean can be, the experience of watching thousands of butterflies flutter among the trees in the Pismo Beach Monarch Butterfly Grove is something that I will never forget.

The Palm, the Pine & Other Important Trees

Signs Now Dot the Historic Highway in Madera

Proposed design of historical marker type sign for Highway 99. Photo: Highway 99 Association

In the Central Valley of California, Highway 99 is the road with a split personality.

One side of that personality is that of the highway many drivers love to hate. While it may be the fastest way to get to and from such Valley cities as Bakersfield, Tulare, Fresno, Madera, Merced or Modesto by car, construction and traffic snarls can ruin the best of plans.

Over the past decade-and-a-half, millions of dollars have poured into the construction of more lanes, better access points, and a variety of other improvements.

The other side of that split personality is the other 99. It is what remains following the major overhaul of the route back in the 1960s. Before the current stretch of concrete, rest stops, and traffic, Highway 99 wound north and south directly through many cities in the Central Valley.

Some of those roads remain in use.

In the City of Merced for example, the original 99 is what we now know as Sixteenth Street. Highway expansion that created the four-lane roadway most of us are familiar with took place decades ago.

The palm and the pine south of Madera on Highway 99. Photo: KCRA Sacramento

The Historic Highway 99 Association of California has sought historic recognition for the highway that was known for a time before Interstate 5 as the transportation backbone of the state.

The Association is looking at local governments that have a portion of the old highway running through their jurisdictions to support efforts to add historic markers along the roadside.

"As we are a new organization and still getting established, what we qualify as a big accomplishment can seem a lot smaller," says Michael Ballard who is president of the Historic Highway 99 Association.

There is a lot of work for this 501(c)3 California Non-Profit Public Benefit Corporation. But the rewards are worth it according to Michael.

The mission of the Association is to make more people aware of the historical significance of the highway. The group points to the iconic palm and pine trees in Madera.

"We are currently working on getting signs posted at the Pine and Palm location along Highway 99," Michael says. "Right now, we are in the early stages of exploring our options as to what we can accomplish."

The palm and the pine represent the geographic center of California. The palm is to the south representing southern California. The pine is to the north representing the northern section of the state.

The exact geographic center is in North Fork in eastern Madera County about fifty miles away from the trees on highway 99.

"We now have a sign design, one for each direction," Michael says. "We are currently working on getting more support for the sign and estimates for its fabrication as well as installation."

Drawing attention to the historical significance of the original highway 99 laid the foundation for the establishment of the

Historic 99 Association. The group received tax-exempt status from the IRS, and can now raise charitable contributions to help achieve goals. The group was successful in 2021 with the completion of a project to get Historic US 99 signs through the city of Madera.

Seven signs were posted along Gateway Drive marking the pre-1958 alignment of US 99 through the city of Madera.

They are building on that effort with the palm and the pine site. The effort requires working with Caltrans, Madera County, and the City of Madera.

In the long term, the organization wants see signs posted on both sides of 99 marking the location of the palm and the pine. The trees are in the median with no safe public access.

The Association hopes it can help secure a State Historic Landmark designation for the site.

"There is a near perfect location for a marker off-site," Michael says.

The Historic Highway 99 Association of California is a Non-Profit Public Benefit Corporation that raises awareness as well as resources to purchase signs and clear government hurdles.

The group's mission as displayed on their website is to *Protect and Promote Historic US 99 in California.*

The challenge now is getting the word out about the group's efforts and goals. With more awareness and increasing membership donations, the group is optimistic it can achieve those goals.

The former roadway once known as Highway 99 is now front and center for the Association. Efforts are being directed toward supporting and protecting the road. The group sees the old highway as a perfect venue for car shows, swap meets, and historical tours.

It may be a long road ahead (pardon the play on words) for this group. But with some early wins such as the sign project in Madera, the future looks promising.

--

The website for Historic Highway 99 can be found at *Historic99.org*

Sequoia Legacy Tree in Visalia

The Sequoia Legacy Tree in Visalia, California. Photo: Steve Newvine

In a sense, this is a story about two guys who shared an office and an idea. It all took place in a small city on the back road to a national park in Central California.

Let's go back to another time. It's wintertime in 1936 in the quaint small city of Visalia, California in Tulare County about forty miles south of Fresno.

Nathan was the Postmaster in a newly opened Visalia Post Office. Guy was the Superintendent of General Grant National Park in the Sierra Mountains. During the winter, the Superintendent shared work space in the post office alongside the Postmaster. In today's office climate, Guy and Nathan would be known as office-mates.

Guy brought two small Sequoia trees to the office one day during that winter season of 1936. Nathan knew there was enough room on the post office property for some unique landscaping. The pair thought re-planting the three-year old trees on opposing sides of the new post office building might give the downtown area a little natural beauty. They also hoped maybe the trees might encourage others to head up into the mountains to see more of the stately trees in the National Park.

The trees grew and grew.

By 1940, General Grant National Park was folded into what we now know as Kings Canyon National Park. The area where visitors can find the General Grant tree is now known as the General Grant Grove.

Nathan and Guy went about their work. Both kept an eye on the post office trees throughout their careers and beyond.

One challenge lingered during the first fifty years the two Sequoias adorned the sides of the Visalia Post Office. One of the trees became diseased and had to be cut down in the mid-1980s.

But the other one continued to grow. Outliving both Nathan and Guy, that tree is now a very special part of the community.

With a history going back to the 1930s, the downtown Visalia Sequoia, better known as the Sequoia Legacy Tree, is a unique part of this city.

In 2018, the City of Visalia formally dedicated the Sequoia Legacy Tree.

The Sequoia Legacy Tree can be found at the corner of Acequia Avenue and Locust Street in Visalia. Photo: Steve Newvine

The Tree is the focal point of a pocket park at the corner of Acequia Avenue and Locust Street in downtown Visalia. Interpretive signs explain the story and get into some of the challenges in the care and feeding of a majestic tree that are normally found in the Sierra Nevada.

The granite pathway the circles the tree is the approximate diameter of the General Sherman Tree in Sequoia National Park. Sequoia National Park is adjacent to Kings Canyon National Park.

This tree has a lot more growing to do.

Keeping the Sequoia Legacy Tree healthy is complicated as it grows on the floor of the San Joaquin Valley far away from the majestic Sierra mountain range.

In the mountains, the sequoias take in water that flows from the snowpack in higher elevations. On the valley floor, the Sequoia Legacy Tree depends on water from the City of Visalia water department. It also depends on the time and attention paid to it from both the public works department and volunteers who keep watchful eyes on any signs of danger that might pose a threat.

There is a sign near the tree reminding visitors that it is really up to each of us to use our water wisely to protect and conserve. That may have been what both Guy and Nathan were thinking back in the mid-1930s when they made it possible for a Sequoia to grow and flourish amidst the sidewalks and tall buildings of downtown Visalia.

Calaveras Big Tree State Park

The California Gold Rush was sparked by the discovery of nuggets in the Sacramento Valley. It put California on the radar of the nation.

When gold was discovered at John Sutter's mill near Coloma in El Dorado County, California in 1848 (the actual year, not 1849 as legend states) the gold rush was on. Soon, the region would fill with prospectors, wannabee gold seekers, and a myriad of service providers.

As news spread of the discovery, thousands of prospective gold miners traveled by sea or over land to San Francisco and the surrounding area. The non-native population of the region exploded from fewer than one-thousand in 1847 to well over one-hundred thousand by 1850.

Resting on a customized park bench as the base of two of the many trees inside Calaveras Big Tree State Park.
Photo: Newvine Personal Collection

While the rush peaked in 1852, some people who look at the era estimate that over two-billion dollars of gold was found during that short period of time.

The rush was effectively over within a few years, but left behind is a beautiful part of the California landscape that visitors now enjoy.

The scenery is spectacular, to coin a word often used by the late *California Gold* television show host Huell Howser. The region lies north of Yosemite National Park in the Sierra Mountains.

Calaveras Big Tree State Park is a free venue that offers small and medium scale hiking paths among the Sequoia trees. The trees are the stars of the show. Looking up in some spaces, it is hard to see the tops of the majestic towers of nature. There are a couple of fallen trees that have been left for visitors to view up close. You get a real idea as to how big these big trees are.

My wife and I posed for a photo in front of the Empire State Tree. As we are transplants from upstate New York, the symbolism of standing next to a tree named for our native state really hit home.

The park had a gift shop that had just the right number of taxidermy wild animals to impress the visitor. My suggestion is to save the gift shop visit until the very end. Otherwise, you might be on the lookout for an angry wildcat or wolf just like the ones preserved for posterity in the gift shop.

There's too much to document in these pages, but permit me to share three venues that have provided natural beauty, with a link to the state's motion picture history, with a little Broadway thrown in.

Railtown 1897 State Historic Park

In Jamestown, Tuolumne County, the Railtown 1897 State Historic Park stands as a monument to western rail history with a nod to the west as depicted in movies and television.

Jamestown is one of the state's original Gold Rush towns. The downtown area includes some old buildings that stood during the mid-eighteen-hundreds and are still in use today.

But the Railtown Park harkens back to the days when the train mastered mass travel. A short ride aboard the restored engine and passenger car takes the traveler further into a relatively small area within the Sierra.

This is not a bullet train. The train moves slowly in part so that the visitor can take in the countryside. The landscape moves by and one can view it all from either inside one of the passenger cars or from the open air car.

Water tower at Railtown 1897 Historic Park in Jamestown, CA
Photo: Newvine Personal Collection

But that's not all. The train and the scenery have been used in dozens of movies and television shows. Movies such as *Unforgiven* with Clint Eastwood shot scenes with the train and surrounding wilderness. The sixties television series *Petticoat Junction* used film shot at the steam engine's water tower.

Railtown also features an authentic engine house when train cars can be maintained. Photo: Newvine Personal Collection

Away from the train station, Railtown Park has displays on how the motion picture industry has shot scenes from classic westerns.

Railtown also displays the engine house for the public to see up close. The engine house is used for maintenance of the rail cars and servicing of the train engine.

There are many old fashioned trains throughout the United States, but Railtown distinguishes itself by a close connection to the movies and television. The folks who really get into trains will appreciate the engine house as it offers a good look at what it takes to keep these classic rail cars in working order.

Columbia

Visitors pan for gold at a prospector's stand in Columbia Historic State Park. Photo: Steve Newvine

In Columbia in Tuolumne County California the rush came. But long after the prospectors left, this little town was not forgotten.

A trip to Columbia can take you back to the Gold Rush days because the town never let go of its history. According to a historical plaque placed by the State Park Commission, Columbia never became a ghost town.

More than five-thousand people lived there in the Gold Rush era. Today, the population stands at just over two-thousand.

Many of the buildings that made up what is now known as Columbia Historic State Park are still standing and still in use. Gold is no longer the big business. Tourism is the draw now with an estimated impact of nearly a quarter billion dollars of annual spending from travelers according to the Visit Tuolumne County 2021 Annual Report (visittuolumne.com).

On a warm sunny day in August, my wife and I took in the village as part of a one-day getaway. Upon parking the car, we were in the historic confines in a matter of minutes.

We watched a pair of blacksmiths pound out customized horseshoes for paying customers. We picked up some chocolate treats from the candy shop. We saw how traditional candles are made at a shop that sells nothing but candles.

We bought lunch at a sit-down saloon with sarsaparilla available upon request. Sarsaparilla was a favored non-alcoholic drink from the Gold Rush era. Fortunately for me on that sunny weekday in that authentic western saloon, other beverages were served as well.

An experience in California's Gold Country does not necessarily need to be restricted to nature. Sierra Repertory Theatre is a local theatre group that has brought Broadway caliber productions, one-person shows, and children's productions to two stages in the region.

Our day was topped off with the Sierra Repertory Theatre's presentation of *Jersey Boys*, the one-time Broadway musical staged during the summer season with professional actors and professional stage personnel. While the show was great, experiencing it inside the historic Fallon House was a capper to a refreshing day of old and new.

The Columbia Historic State Park was created in 1945. It was established by the state to preserve the historic buildings. Some eight decades later, it remains very much like it was back in the Gold Rush era.

The region around Columbia was known as the southern mines as it lies well south of Sutter's Mill where the first discovery of gold took place. For people living in the Merced and Atwater side of the County, you can get there within an hour and a half.

My wife and I have used Columbia as a convenient one-day event destination for out-of-town visitors. It is another side to California that sometimes gets lost in the common misconceptions of the state being only about San Francisco or Los Angeles.

There's a lot of history up there, and thankfully a lot of it has stayed in place ready to be rediscovered.

Gold country has a lot to offer the visitor to the region as well at the Californian who might be considering a change of scenery. It's a place with clean air, a semblance of four seasons, and a difference pace in everyday life.

The San Joaquin Sound

Buckaroo Reunion

(Top) the Buckaroos then with Buck Owens, and now(bottom) carrying on his legacy. Photo: Buck Owens Private Foundation

Over fifty years ago, Fresno musician Jim Shaw wanted to record his country band *Nashville West* in a new studio owned by the legendary Buck Owens in Bakersfield.

Little did he know he would meet Buck and be asked to record with him that very day.

"Buck was recording and needed a piano player. He was told there was a piano player in the building: me."

While Owens did not know Jim, he came out of the studio to meet him and asked whether Jim could play in the session. Jim looked at the music, and then told Buck he would handle the rather complicated chord changes. Buck took a chance and used Jim for the session.

That session worked out, and would soon be followed by a few more before Buck asked Jim if he'd like to join the group.

"By June of 1970, I was hired as a member of the Buckaroos," Jim said.

The Buckaroos with Dean Martin in a photograph from the 1970s. Buck Owens and the Buckaroos appeared on a number of TV variety shows in the seventies including the Ed Sullivan Show, Glen Campbell Goodtime Hour and Martin's program. Photo: Buck Owens Private Foundation

Jim has been part of the Buckaroos ever since. He played in the band during the *Hee Haw* TV show that Buck co-hosted with Roy Clark. Jim was there for the road appearances, network variety shows, and in the recording studio.

He never left the group.

Band members moved on over the years and were replaced by other musicians. Jim along with Doyle Curtsinger, who joined shortly before Jim, have both remained with the band for over fifty years.

The Central Valley's country music heritage was on full display on the stage of the Buck Owens Crystal Palace in Bakersfield in late March of 2023.

The Buckaroos performed for the first time since COVID restrictions closed the place back in 2020.

While the Palace would reopen once restrictions were lifted, the band went into a sort of holding pattern.

Jim Shaw on the keyboards at the Buckaroos reunion shows at the Crystal Palace in Bakersfield. Photo: Steve Daniels

Buck Owens died in 2005, but the band continued performing at the Crystal Palace.

Jim has played with the Buckaroos along with serving as the managing director for the Buck Owens Private Foundation. The Foundation runs the entertainment, publishing, and recording arms of the singer's estate.

When he signed on, he joined legendary guitarist Don Rich and bass player Doyle Holly who were stalwarts of the band. Holly left a year later to forge a solo career. Rich died in a car accident in 1974.

There were others who became Buckaroos over the past five decades. So the reunion shows took on a special significance. Also on stage for the reunion was lead singer Buckaroo Kim McAbee. On her Facebook page, she said of the reunion, "So much fun with the Buckaroos together again after three years."

Jim Shaw echoed the sentiments of Kim and others by saying the two shows at the Crystal Palace went very well. "Friday night was totally sold out and we had an enthusiastic crowd and a train-wreck free performance."

When he met Buck more than five decades ago Jim had no idea how his life would change. "I moved into running Buck's recording studio and took on other duties over the years. I've been a managing director of the Buck Owens Private Foundation for the past seventeen years."

Jim describes recording for Buck as an experience that was at times challenging but also inspiring. "It was interesting," he says of those years. "Buck was a perfectionist. On the other hand, he brought out the best of us."

The Buckaroos band was considered one of the best instrumental groups in country music. That's due in part to that hard-driving leadership from Buck Owens and in part to the musical magic that can happen many times within a small band. Each member brings in something unique, and when the conditions are right, the results can be magical.

Buck Owens and the *Buckaroos* were co-founders of the so-called *Bakersfield Sound*, a distinctive style of country music that focused on a smaller number of musicians and the liberal use of electric guitars. Buck Owens and Merle Haggard were the best known country artists who delivered the *Bakersfield Sound*.

Behind those two country icons were the back-up bands. Haggard had the *Strangers*. Owens had the *Buckaroos*.

"Back in our heyday, every major country artist had their own band," Jim said. "Loretta Lynn had the *Coal Miners*, and Johnny Cash originally had the *Tennessee Two*. Now, an artist may have a band, but often the faces change, and rarely are they even named."

It is different for the *Buckaroos*. They keep the flame burning.

Thanks to reunion shows like the two performed in late March in Bakersfield, the *Buckaroos* continue to keep the *Bakersfield Sound* alive.

The Night Kenny Rogers Came to the Central Valley

Country/pop star Kenny Rogersat the Merced Theatre October 2014. Photo: Merced Theatre Foundation

Few people who were in audience that night will forget the songs, the singer, or the long road it took to make it happen.

When Kenny Rogers sang the lyrics to his hit song *The Gambler*, "You've got to know when to hold them", in a Central Valley show back in October of 2014, it was just another packed house for the entertainer.

But it was a big deal for this medium-sized city (population 80,000) to host the singer.

The marquee at the Merced Theatre points out that over one-thousand tickets were sold for the October 2014 concert by Kenny Rogers. Photo: Merced Theatre Foundation

At the time, the historic Merced Theatre had completed renovations. A number of lesser known musical acts had taken to the stage, but landing this Grammy and Country Music Association award winning artist was both a coup and a risk.

The questions raised at the time Kenny was booked included: Would the crowds show up? Would the show be a success? As it would turn out, those fears about whether audiences would respond were erased.

"The Theatre re-opened after renovations in April 2012," said managing director Heather Holt. "Kenny was our first sold out show."

Necola Adams remembers the night she met Kenny Rogers following that performance in Merced.

"We shook hands," she said. "He had the softest hands I've ever touched." Necola, who owns Mrs. Adams Gourmet Cookies in Merced, had taken six dozen of her cookies to Kenny's road manager.

The manager asked her to wait until the show was over so that he could introduce her to his boss. "I heard the whole show from inside Kenny's tour bus," she said.

Necola Adams with Kenny Rogers. Photo: Necola Adams

After the show, Nicola was the first person Kenny met as security escorted him from the stage to his bus. Following an introduction by the road manager, Kenny suggested a photo opportunity. "I was the only person to get a picture taken with him," she said.

Kenny Rogers had a career in music that dated back to the late 1950s. In the 1960s, he was the lead singer for the rock group *First Edition* (later to be called *Kenny Rogers and the First Edition*).

The group disbanded in the seventies and Kenny pursued a solo career in country music.

He had a number of hit records in that decade including the iconic story song *The Gambler*. That record sold three-million copies, led to a TV-movie career, and made him an arena-packing performer.

In 1983, he teamed with Dolly Parton for the song *Islands in the Stream*. That hit record cemented his place in Country and Pop music. In the nineties and into the 2000s, he continued performing and releasing new music sporadically.

Then in the early twenty-teens he accepted the opportunity to play The Art Kamangar Center at The Merced Theatre. By the time the Merced Theater show, he was just a few months away from announcing the start of a farewell tour.

"He was the first really big name to come to the Theatre since the renovation," Heather Holt said.

That farewell tour started in 2015 and ended in 2018 with an announcement he would end performing on stage based on advice from his doctors.

A bladder cancer diagnosis led to his decision to end his touring.

He died in hospice care on March 20, 2020.

Nicola hangs on to pleasant memories of how nice he treated her right after his Merced show. "You can meet some really nice people if you don't act crazy around them," she said. "He was a genuinely nice guy."

Bob Hope Theatre

The official logo of the Bob Hope Theatre in Stockton, CA. Image: BobHopeTheatre.com

While younger people may have never heard of him, to millions of Americans the name Bob Hope conjures up laughs and lightheartedness.

Earlier generations recall the television specials and the comedian entertaining military troops at Christmastime from years ago.

The City of Stockton holds the distinction of being home to a performing arts venue named in honor of the beloved entertainer. Thanks to the generosity of the late Stockton property developer Alex Spanos, the Hope name lives on in that city of over a quarter-million people about fifty miles south of Sacramento.

The *Bob Hope Theatre* opened in the early 2000s in a refurbished Fox Theatre in downtown Stockton. The building was almost lost to the wrecking ball when Spanos stepped forward with an idea to honor his friend, and a checkbook.

Alex Spanos was good friends with Bob Hope. Here, the pair performed a soft-shoe dance routine for a charity function. Photo: AGSpanos.com

Spanos was primarily known as the owner of the National Football League's San Diego Chargers. The Chargers are now based in Los Angeles, In the City of Stockton, Alex Spanos was a property developer and community philanthropist. He passed away in 2018.

The Spanos name graces high school football fields, a college performing arts center, hospital wings and other places throughout the City of Stockton. In addition, there are scholarship endowments, charity golf tournaments and art exhibits that have been underwritten by the Spanos family.

The company website has a special section on the Spanos commitment to charitable giving not only in the Central Valley, but up and down the state of California and into the state of Nevada.

Around the turn of the century, Alex Spanos was able to mesh his desire to give more to the City of Stockton with the admiration of his then thirty-year friendship with comedian Bob Hope.

He gave a half-million dollar gift to the organization handling the rehabilitation of a former vaudeville theater and asked that the building be named after his friend. That's how the *Bob Hope Theatre* in downtown Stockton got the name.

Bob Hope and Alex Spanos became friends following a charity golf function in 1969. "Bob and I teamed up against Bing Crosby and his partner and we beat them," Spanos said in an interview with television station KCRA in Sacramento well over a decade ago, "From that day onward, Bob and I played golf practically every week."

The friendship grew over the years with Hope participating in charity events alongside Spanos. The comedian was an occasional visitor to the owner's box at Charger games in San Diego. Bob Hope died in 2003 at the age of 100.

The theater site started as the T & D Photoplay in 1916, hosting vaudeville and other entertainment acts. It was renamed the California five years later. The building was torn down at the start of the Great Depression.

The Fox California opened on the site in 1930. During the 1930's, big stars such as Al Jolson and the Marx Brothers performed there. As vaudeville was replaced by radio as America's primary source of entertainment, the Fox California relied on moviegoers as a primary source of revenue.

In 1973, the theater closed. The building was placed on the *National Register of Historic* Places in the late 1970's. The City and its' Redevelopment Agency included the theater in a revitalization plan in the early 1990's.

By the early 2000's, a combination of the Spanos donation and government funds saved the project and resulted in the renovation that residents and others enjoy today.

For a few years following the comedian's death, there was an online tribute to the friendship shared between Bob Hope and Alex Spanos. On the company website at that time, there was special section where a video of a soft-shoe dance routine with Spanos and Hope was featured. It is not too often you see a world renowned entertainer alongside one of California's most generous men take to a stage to wow an audience.

You can find a brief section of the video on YouTube. It is no longer available on the AGSpanos.com site. Alex Spanos carried himself pretty well as a soft-shoe dancer, while Bob Hope showed that he still had the goods in his late eighties at the time of the video (circa 1980).

The comedian likely knew his friend was responsible for the renaming of the theater. Bob Hope passed away a year before the official grand opening. According to the theatre website, the comedian never performed there in the previous iterations of the venue.

The *Bob Hope Theatre* was among the first California entertainment venues to reopen after the worst of the COVID pandemic. Audiences that assemble beneath the ornate chandelier inside the historic building may not know that much about the comedian's legacy.

But thanks to the half-million dollar gift from his friend AG Spanos, and the vision of community members who would not let the wrecking ball take down the building, the Hope name remains part of the history of the Central Valley.

Building Greatness

The View from the Top of an Iconic Courthouse

On the left - The view looking down N Street from on top of the Merced County Courthouse Museum. Right: The exterior of the iconic building. Photos: Steve Newvine

Many communities in California have taken advantage of repurposing aging government buildings to new uses.

In the City of Merced, an old County Courthouse building was turned over to the County historical society as a museum and repository of local history.

The building, with an iconic cupola, stands proudly over this community. There have been many times over the years when the thought of what the view might look like from that vantage point has crossed many a curious observer.

Visually, this is one of the most interesting stories I have had the opportunity to write over the past several years.

"The cupola is a restricted area and is full of cobwebs and dead bees," County Historian Sarah Lim warned when I made the request to get the insider's view from the cupola.

When the day finally arrived, she told me she would unlock the door and let me go up alone.

Once I started up the narrow stairway, I understood why. I wiped cobwebs off my clothes, and started taking pictures.

As I made my way to the first level of the cupola, I took in the view from all four sides. From here looking down N Street, I could see downtown Merced.

Going clockwise, I saw the roof of the County Library, the top of the Sheriff's Department, and completed the circle with a view of Merced Police Headquarters leading to the traffic signal on M Street.

The area within this footprint comprises the Courthouse Neighborhood. It is one of the oldest neighborhoods in the City of Merced. In the late 1800s and early 1900s, it was a dynamic community with nice homes and offices.

With the passing of time, most of the homes have been converted either to offices or multi-unit apartments. It is still a nice neighborhood, but there have been changes that align with the movement of population to newer homes with closer proximity to retailing.

Access to the upper, non-public floors of the Courthouse museum begin with this locked staircase off the third floor, followed by a winding set of stairs that eventually lead to the top. Photos: Steve Newvine

Three sides of the cupola overlook statues of the Roman Goddess Justica. According to information provided to me from County Historian Lim, the statues represent justice. But as the architect did not believe justice is blind, he chose not to depict the Goddess as blind.

According to the architectural history, the statues are made out of redwood, are hand-carved and are approximately twice life-size. The statue at the very top of the cupola is Minerva, the Roman Goddess of Wisdom. There were deliberate architectural and stylistic choices, along with a good deal of symbolism behind the look of the Courthouse.

From the relatively plain look on the ground level, to the more ornate styles heading up to the higher floors, the architect designed the building to communicate a sense of enlightenment as the visitor moved up through the structure.

From the upper level of the structure, lots of daylight fills the cupola. Photo: Steve Newvine

While the view was great, the highest level was worth risking my fear of heights. Up one final spiral set of stairs and I was now standing in the top level of the cupola. Only the Goddess Minerva stood higher: outside on the dome. The height from the ground to the very top of the dome is just under one-hundred, six feet.

On a clear day, we're told you can see the entire County. My visit took place in late August in the midst of the heatwave and in skies filled with pollutants from the California wildfires in the region.

This indoor adventure was all worth the trouble: getting special permission, enduring the cobwebs and navigating dead bees as well as live spiders.

This is the view from the cupola on top of the Merced County Courthouse Museum. The statue is of the Roman Goddess Justica, but without the blindfold. This was a creative choice by the building architect who, according to the history of the building, did not believe justice is blind. Photo: Steve Newvine

As our community continues to evolve and change in the coming decades, it will likely look pretty much the same from five stories up in the Merced County Courthouse Museum building.

Traffic Circles and Straight Lines-Roundabouts

Roundabouts are prominent along the Campus Parkway connecting Highway 99 to the UC Merced campus. Photo: Steve Newvine

When a visitor to the University of California at Merced campus shared her story about driving one-hundred miles from the Bay Area to this medium-sized Central Valley city, she honed in on one unique characteristic of a new highway in the community.

"I've never seen so many traffic circles for such a short distance."

The highway she was referencing was the latest extension of the Campus Parkway project.

The roadway has the appearance of a beautiful, almost pristine, asphalt pathway that connects California Highway

99 to just south of the UC Merced Campus. The road is a true connection of the 99 Freeway to the University.

"Government should and can do the big things," Merced County Supervisor Josh Pedrozo said at the ceremony marking the opening of the roadway in July 2022. He represents the district where the new highway is located.

The one-hundred million dollar price tag is paid for from state dollars that matched local tax revenues from a locally approved sales tax hike earmarked for roads. The transportation bill that secured the funding was cited by local leaders as an excellent example of legislators working across the aisle on behalf of their constituents.

This highway expansion includes the addition of roundabouts at some of the intersections. These are junctions where traffic moves in one direction around a central island to reach one of the roads that meet the intersection.

They are also known as traffic circles. "When roundabouts started showing up in road projects, I hated them," said then County Board of Supervisors Chairman Lloyd Pareira. "But now I like them. They keep the traffic moving."

The newly opened section completes the south-eastern portion of the so-called "Merced Loop System." That loop system will one day run south of the City of Merced and connect with the City of Atwater.

Campus Parkway will help take traffic to and from the university. It will also help better connect traffic to Yosemite National Park.

Another special feature of the Campus Parkway is the bicycle/pedestrian pathway that runs along the western side of the highway.

The view from the new bike/pedestrian bridge over the Olive Avenue roundabout section of Campus Parkway.

The path includes an overpass at Olive Avenue so that cyclists, runners, and walkers may avoid crossing the street at grade level. The path helps soften concerns about road expansion projects taking away some of the quality of life issues neighbors around the area might have been inclined to raise.

Local leaders say a lot of good has come about as the result of this one-hundred million dollar investment in the community. With the bike path, the highway combines functionality with recreation.

A highway such as this is a big win for the community. But for visitors from other parts of the state, it is just a connector from the main highway to the University. A connector with a couple of traffic circles mixed in to give visitors something to talk about when they reach their intended destination.

Rebuilding a Historic Theater

*Merced Theatre. Merced California.
Photo: Steve Newvine*

There was a time in California where entertainment was found on the stages of theaters throughout the cities of the state.

Back in the 1920s and 1930s, vaudeville provided the opportunity for people to go out and see a show at the local theater or opera house.

Vaudeville was ushered out and the growing industry of motion pictures became the gathering place for people seeking entertainment. The heyday of the movies was the 1940s. Flickering off on the sidelines was the new medium of television.

In the 1950s, TV dominated the living rooms, leaving the theaters to try gimmicks such as 3D, *CinemaScope*, or some other enhancements to bring people back. It was during this period of time theaters, especially the movie houses, began a decline.

By the 1970s, shopping malls with their multi-screen theaters put the final nail in the movie house coffin. Pictures were still being made, but television was the primary delivery mode for entertainment.

The grand movie theaters from the golden age were either torn down, converted to some other use, or left to decay.

In the case of the Merced Theatre in this Central Valley city, there were a handful of visionaries who put action behind their dreams.

A non-profit foundation was formed, fund raisers were held, leadership gifts were sought, legislative grants were awarded and a little luck was found.

In about ten years from those early dreams, the community was welcomed to a newly remodeled theater. Named after the local philanthropist who made a substantial gift, the *Art Kammager Theatre* now showcases local musical talent, brings in regional and national musical artists for concerts, and provides a venue for award ceremonies and the fall semester graduation ceremony for the University of California at Merced.

Shortly after the reopening, the community was invited to see all it took to make this dream come true.

For the first time, we were able to walk all over the place.

Our backstage pass was a community wide invitation to stop in during a three-hour Sunday afternoon window.

We were allowed to view many areas of the theater that the public ordinarily does not get a chance to see. With

Foundation members sprinkled all over the place to answer questions to give us directions, we took the self-guided tour.

We entered through the main entrance underneath the marquee. The smell of popcorn set just the right mood for touring a movie theater

From there, it was on to the stage where we could see the audience seating from the perspective of a performer. The house lights that illuminated the audience seating may not have been the same as a spotlight shining in the eyes of a performer, but it was still a treat to be on stage.

The wings of the stage are reminiscent of the wings of any high school auditorium stage. There was even a spiral stairway that could take a stagehand all the way to the ceiling if the production called for that task. The spiral stairway was not open to the public.

Like many venue's the Merced Theatre's Green Room is not painted green. A green room is where performer's prepare for their entrance on-stage during a performance. Photo: Steve Newvine

A Theatre volunteer told us how to go downstairs to the green room and the dressing rooms where the performers get ready for a performance. The green room (the name goes back to theater legend, but this room was actually painted beige) is where a performer who is not needed at a particular time during the performance waits until he or she is called on stage.

There are two dressing rooms; each with a glittery star on door. Both dressing rooms had bathrooms and showers. You can imagine the performers nervously awaiting their call to come upstairs to the wings of the stage.

There's a video camera shooting the stage, and the video feed is wired to the green room area.

Our back stage tour of the Merced Theatre made for a fun Sunday afternoon in our city. But throughout California, there are dozens of restored theaters that offer all kinds of entertainment. They are treasures of architecture, a repository of show business history from the state, and an interesting place to hang out for a couple of hours prior to a show.

The real entertainment however, is on stage from the vantage point of the audience seating.

Giving People

Kettle Stories- Seasonal Tradition Began in Bay Area

The Salvation Army sets up Red Kettles at a number of area businesses during the Christmas season. Photo: Steve Newvine

When the Christmas holiday season arrives, many retailers step up their community service to help their customers and those in need.

That's certainly the case to the many stores that welcome the red kettle.

Salvation Army has a core of paid workers, augmented by scores of volunteers, ringing the bell and raising money for the organization.

The tradition of the red kettle and the bell ringing started in the Bay Area of California over one-hundred, thirty years ago.

The local Salvation Army Captain there was saddened to see so many poor families having a hard time during the holiday season. This Captain wanted to give every struggling family a Christmas dinner.

His problem: finding money to pay for everything.

After many sleepless nights, this Captain remembered the so called Simpson's Pot near a naval docking site. The Pot was for the collection of loose coins anyone passing by might have for the poor.

The Captain copied that idea and placed a pot at the Oakland Ferry Landing on Market Street in San Francisco. The rest is history.

Major Turnie Wright of the Merced chapter of Salvation Army says the campaign is a highly visible focal point for the organization. "We saw 2021 as a hiccup year as the pandemic was winding down. But there was and still is today a need to help those in need."

In addition to the kettles, Salvation Army has Angel Trees in a handful of businesses where a shopper can pick an angel from a Christmas tree, and then shop for a particular toy written on that angel.

The benefits from the annual campaign go well beyond the recipients of the holiday food and toys. There are many touching stories heard by the people who ring the bell at kettle locations.

One woman with a British accent called the organization the "Sally Army" explaining that the moniker was used back in Great Britain where she lived as a child. "They (Salvation Army) had a great band that I remember hearing every Christmas. It was a wonderful tradition."

A man shared the story about how he was helped by the Salvation Army many years ago when he had fallen on hard times. "I promised myself then that once I got back on my feet, I would never forget what they did for me."

Major Wright has some of his own stories about people touched by the Red Kettle Campaign. He worked the kettle at a grocery store where he would sing instead of ring a bell. A woman walked by and told him she'd be right back. She came back later with a small stocking that she knitted in her car. "She enjoyed the singing instead of the bell and wanted to give," the Major said. "But at that stage she did not have any other cash on her. So she knitted the small stocking."

The Major related a story about meeting a young child who had a *McDonalds Happy Meal*. The child took the toy out of her *Happy Meal* box and asked that it be given to a young child that did not have anything.

Stories of generosity among givers have touched Major Wright and his team over the years. "These small gifts stand out the most in my mind," he said. "It was attitude of the giver giving the gift that just made my day."

The Red Kettle started right here in California well over a century ago, and the need still exists for the many struggling families. Each family has a story.

The folks who help out the Salvation Army can tell their own stories about how a smile and the cling of a tiny bell has made an impact on their own lives.

Non-Profits Bottom Line Pop from Fireworks Sales

The fireworks stand benefiting Playhouse Merced is in a grocery store parking lot Merced, CA. Photo: Steve Newvine

The Independence Day holiday brings out the best in our celebratory spirit when it comes to showing our love of country.

Flags are waving, some communities have parades, hot dogs will be grilling, and many will take in the sense of pride for the good things about the United States.

In California, add to that list the sale of fireworks.

The Merced Marching 100 benefits from fireworks sales from a prime location in the Merced Mall parking lot on Olive Avenue. Photo: Steve Newvine

The stands are sprinkled throughout the state. Working with the fireworks wholesalers, non-profit organizations apply for permits, staff the booths, and raise a big portion of their annual budgets.

That's how it's done in California. "We have had a fireworks booth for 10 years or more," a spokesperson for Playhouse Merced says. The Playhouse is a non-profit organization that staffs the booth in the parking lot at a grocery store.

The wholesalers coordinate the paperwork to secure the permits. The non-profit organization agrees to abide by the local rules governing the sale of the product.

Fire safety is part of the arrangement with the fireworks being stored in large metal storage containers that are near every stand. In exchange for agreeing to abide by the rules, the non-profit and their volunteers staff the booth right on through the July 4th holiday.

The profits are sizable, and the wholesaler takes back any unsold inventory. "It does provide a large part of our operating income for our Youth Educational programs and our Community Theatre Live Productions," the spokesperson for Playhouse Merced said.

Customers can spend upwards of one-hundred dollars for the so-called "safe and sane" fireworks. There are bigger boxes offering a variety of neighborhood-ready fireworks that sell anywhere from two-hundred to four-hundred dollars a box.

Most of the cities in Merced County handle the permitting and inspection of the fireworks booths through the local fire department. Merced County Fire performs this role in areas where either the city does not handle this role.

It's a big commitment for a non-profit organization to commit their volunteers and staff to working a shift at a fireworks stand. From my experience running a non-profit some fifteen years ago, it seemed as though the volunteers were eager to do a good job.

The staff did their best to pull a shift here and there while continuing to do their real jobs for the organization.

I recall doing an analysis of the profit versus expenses following the fireworks stand effort my non-profit organization operated back in 2006.

Some communities in northern California no longer permit sales of safe-and-sane fireworks due to the wildfire threats in recent years. The City of Redding in northern California does not allow fireworks sales. City Manager Barry Tippen says the City has maintained this policy for the past several years.

Some of the local sellers will have a close-out sale on July 5, but by the end of the week, most of the stands will have been taken down and shipped back to the wholesaler's storage sites. Another fireworks season will close.

That is unless some folks have put some of their fireworks away for a special occasion sometime over the next twelve months.

Flood Relief-
Filling a Sandbag of Hope

Volunteers staffed the Love INC portable shower ministry that was moved to the County Fairgrounds where a shelter for evacuated residents was set up. In Atwater, volunteers moved quickly to fill sandbags for residents needing them.
Photo: Love INC and City of Atwater Facebook pages.

Merced Mayor Matthew Serrato had one hope as the New Year was about to begin. His wish: "I just want to see work get done."

In January of 2023, storms struck the city and surrounding areas. The community went through a lot as a result of the powerful rains and winds.

The week of January 9 will stand out as a week when the brutality of the weather was overpowered only by the capacity of first responders and volunteers to step up to help their neighbors.

On Monday, residents near the Bear Creek area were evacuated to shelters set up at the Merced County Fairgrounds. A day later, the entire community of Planada was evacuated.

From the very beginning, the community stepped in to help.

Love INC, a coalition of local faith communities, brought their portable shower ministry to the Fairgrounds. Ordinarily, the showers are offered at an area homeless shelter. This time around, the showers were available to anyone, including the families that were evacuated.

In Atwater, the City's Facebook page described the outpouring of help from neighbors simply as "community helping one another". Volunteers filled sand bags and helped out wherever they were needed.

Even students at Our Lady of Mercy School in Catholic got into the spirit of helping. They filled sandbags for distribution to any homeowner who needed them.

The entire city of Planada, some four-thousand residents, was evacuated as rain and wind devastated everything within the confines of city limits.

Stores were damaged. Homes were mucked up with water and mud. But the people came, rolled up their sleeves, and got down to work.

Lots of individuals and organizations held fundraisers to turn over money to the agencies working on restoring the community back to what it was like before the floods. An advertising specialties company printed special tee shirts for sale with the proceeds going to Planada.

On the campus at a local college in the late spring of 2023, a 5K run was organized to raise money for a community in need. A few hundred runners, supporters, and volunteers took part and turned over about eight-thousand dollars to help the people who needed a lift out of the devastation that overtook their community earlier in the year.

The County of Merced provided some of the amazing aerial photography of the devastating January 2023 floods. The County set up a special storm information link on the County website and asked residents to donate supplies to three flood shelters. Within days, the shelters were stocked. Photo: Merced County Facebook page.

People from all over the Merced area came in once the first wave of danger had eased off. The floors of the Planada Community Church were covered with rain water. Sacred Heart Church in the city collected donations of blankets and other needed supplies, working in conjunction with Catholic Charities of Merced County.

Within a few days, the evacuation order was lifted. The County thanked the community and reported that all shelters were fully stocked with essentials to help families get back to normal.
It was a trying time for Merced County in the Central Valley and for much of the state of California. The silver lining in

these storm clouds has been the willingness of so many people to donate money, goods, and time.

That includes the group of running athletes, casual runners, walkers, children, and even a few dogs that trained in the weeks leading up to the community fund raiser. Most were satisfied that they made it to the finish line. Everyone was pleased to know they played a small part in an initiative to make a big impact in their community.

Planada Gets Help

Fernando Nava looks out to a field some 500-feet away from his home. Photo: Steve Newvine

Fernando Nava is thankful.

"We've been working together, my family and neighbors, and putting it all back together."

Fernando's family made Planada their home many years ago. So when the devastating January 2023 flood waters ravaged their community, there was no second thought about moving away and starting over.

"My brother and my father live right here on the same street," he said. "We all did what we had to do to bring everything back."

Flood waters from the mid-January rains covered the entire city of four-thousand. Everyone was evacuated and many have still not been able to live in their homes.

Residents in Planada are now putting water damaged furniture and building materials on the curb for pick up by County crews taking it all to a landfill. Photo: Steve Newvine

The City's Community Center became a hub for a variety of services to help residents. Salvation Army had a Food Distribution truck there. The Billy Graham Evangelistic Association set up shop with construction help for homeowners. A portable washer and dryer truck was hooked up in a parking lot. Sixteen machines were running practically all day long.

Pallets of water, clean-up chemicals, and other supplies were available from the same parking lot. Hot meals were served at least twice a day. Residents could drive up to a volunteer pop up tent and pick up meals.

Fernando pointed out how high the water rose at the worst point during that week of January 16. At his home, the water was at least a foot deep inside the house.

There's a telltale sign of just how high the water got: water stains on the front of houses. "We've gotten some prices on just replacing our kitchen cabinets and countertop," Fernando said. "We're looking at nine-thousand dollars, and that's just for the basic set up."

Some residents have flood insurance, but others like Fernando are relying on the help of the agencies that have come to town with assistance.

But he has family and friends who can help him and who he can assist as well. For that, he is grateful.

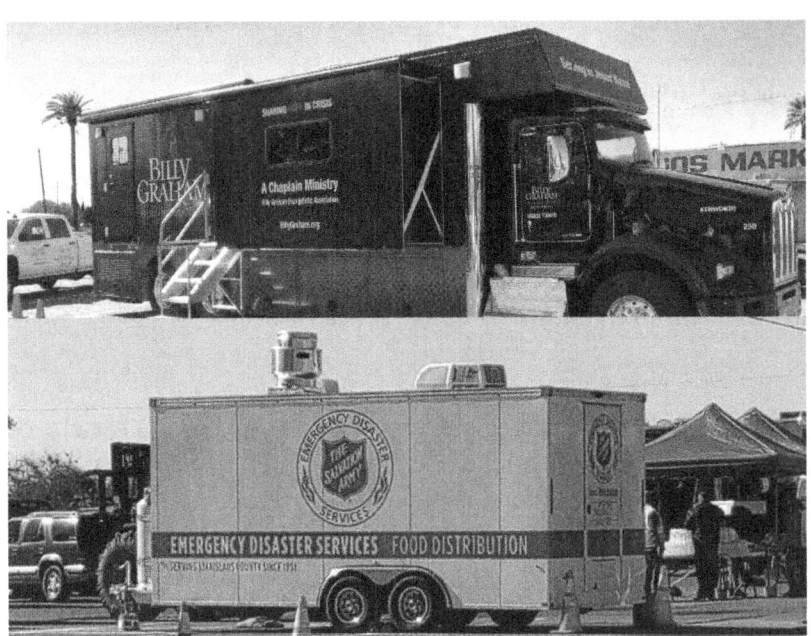

The Billy Graham Evangelistic Association (top) and the Salvation Army (bottom) had a big presence in the community of Planada. Other organizations include Federal Emergency Management Administration (FEMA), Small Business Administration, area churches, and local government among many others. Photos: Steve Newvine

Fernando has been taken back by the outpouring of resources coming to the aid of Planada and other flooded regions of the state. "People are not forgetting Planada," he said.

He feels it has been a true community effort, not only in Merced County, but throughout the state and the federal government.

Businesses would eventually reopen. In those early weeks following the storms, a sound of construction work permeating the community could be heard. Little by little, life was returning to normal.

Seven months later, officials and community members gathered at the Planada Community Center to celebrate a reopening.

The Center was heavily damaged in the flooding, but a speedy turnaround of insurance claims brought together over four-hundred thousand dollars that was put to use to complete renovations.

Things were looking up.

For Fernando and many others, there was light at the end of those once dark days.

Summer School

Incoming sophomores, juniors, and seniors took part in the six week Summer Prep Academy. Photo: Steve Newvine

School students often find that their adventures on the back roads in the summer are tempered with some classroom time.

Summer school is part of the routine for many.

When I was in grade school, one of the first questions asked on the first day of class was "What did you do on vacation?"

In 2022, I spent part of my summer with a group of high school students in an enrichment program held on the UC Merced Campus.

The program was called the High School Summer Prep Academy. It was a program of the Harvest Park Educational Center, a non-profit based in Merced.

Harvest Park Education Center was created to provide at-risk, disconnected, and poverty stricken children and older youth with supplemental education and new information to build on their basic skills.

The summer academy is the creation of Gloria Morris. She is an educator who has been developing programs to help youth overcome the obstacles they face growing up and, in turn, provide an opportunity for these youth to prepare themselves for higher education and the workforce.

During the six week session, incoming high school students were given a review of basic math, sentence structure, and parts of speech. The four-hour, daily lessons included opportunities to explore career choices that the students were passionate about pursuing.

And there were guest speakers. That's where I came in. I was approached by Gloria and her husband Robert to consider presenting a few lectures on my professional career and how higher education helped open doors for me to get better opportunities throughout my forty-year working career

The three of us developed a three-unit set of lectures on college preparedness. I provided insight on my career achievements, Robert showed the students how to research their career areas of interest, and Gloria presented sessions on her Principles Based Lifestyle Training or PBLT.

PBLT is an evidenced based learning curriculum developed by Gloria that focuses on the development of a strong academic foundation.

In the first of my three meetings with the class, I told my story about being the first in my family to graduate from college. I connected my education and work experiences to the success I achieved over four decades.

My second meeting with the group provided an opportunity to offer suggestions on how to succeed academically. I used real examples from my experiences as well as the experiences of friends and colleagues.

The third and final session was about soft skills. Soft skills are the work habits, communication strategies, and people skills an employee can develop to help succeed at work. The source of the session was my 2009 book *Soft Skills for Hard Times*.

It meant a lot to me to be able to share my experiences with this group. Based on their feedback, their questions during the sessions, and their participation in the training, the program succeeded on many levels.

Those levels would include the refresher sessions on math, language skills, and basic writing. We can all use a refresher on those topics from time to time.

It was good for the group to see adults who have enjoyed some measure of success in their lives come into a classroom and share their experiences. From my own experiences growing up, a real person doing a real job always made an impression.

It was also a plus to have the sessions on the UC Merced campus. The sprawling array of buildings, athletic fields, and parking lots might serve to inspire many to see beyond the confines of their home and school.

So the answer to the question "what did you do this summer" can be answered by the participants of this program with a simple response.

"I went back to school to learn a little about the real world."

A Community Tragedy

Photo: GoFundMe.com

It's the ugly underside of life in a smaller community along the California back roads. The brutal murder and robbery of four family members grabbed the headlines.

Still, it is a story that needs to be told.

Merced was a community in mourning in the autumn of 2022.

We lost four souls in what prosecutors believe to be a greed fueled robbery and kidnapping.

A mother, father, infant child, and one other family member were killed. Two men are in jail where they face a lifetime of incarceration.

The Singh family worked their business, raised their children, and had every hope of a life filled with earthly blessings Those plans came to a frightening end when the four family members were forcibly taken from their business. Within hours, the four were murdered.

Killed were Aroohi Dheri, her mother Jasleen Kaur, father Jasdeep Singh and her uncle Amandeep Singh.

Suspect Jesus Manuel Salgado was arrested. His brother Albert was arrested a short time later. They face kidnapping and murder charges.

This community will never forget. Local faith communities presided over four days of memorial services held in downtown Merced. The four nights of vigils represented the four victims of this crime. While there are four victims, that number is much higher when considering the surviving family members, the business associates, neighbors, friends, and others who were touched by the lives of the family.

Within days of the news, over four-thousand families, individuals, and businesses donated well over four-hundred thousand dollars to the surviving family members through a Go-Fund-Me solicitation.

According to the description on the Go Fund Me site, the family "worked tirelessly for 18 years to achieve safety, security, and community for themselves and their families. Aman and Jasdeep were the primary wage earners for the family, supported their elderly parents, and lived under one roof."

Aroohi Dheri, her parents, and uncle. Photos: Go Fund Me

The page goes on to explain how Jasdeep (also known as JB) and Jaeleen were married in India in 2019. She joined her husband in the US one year after their marriage once her immigration was finalized. Baby Aroohi was just eight months old.

JB's brother Aman was married and had two children ages six and nine.

When a hard working family can be taken away (based on security cameras that captured the kidnapping) in broad daylight, many are within their rights to wonder whether the same thing could happen to them.

But underneath all of this is hope. With memorials springing up almost immediately, and an overwhelming response to a crowdfunding drive, it is clear our community is speaking with actions.

These actions include the messages on social media offering prayers and support for the Dheri family. As local citizen Raj Sidhu wrote: "That is a great example of a great community and the outpouring of love for the Sikh community. I will keep praying for Merced" Raj speaks well for how many feel during this troubling time.

Our community witnessed this incredible chain of events started with the horrible crime.

But we also saw a community of compassion play out during the four memorial services for the victims. The response to a call for help for the surviving family members is nothing short of astounding. All of this originated in the same community where tragedy struck.

So we have had some bad in this community, but we have seen a lot of good as well. Maybe that bodes well for the future.

We may be a little off our game right now, but we will be coming back soon to continue celebrating the good things about life in our community.

A Bite to Eat

Josh's Favorite Eatery- Wool Growers Restaurant Enjoyed by NFL Greats Madden and Allen

Buffalo Bills quarterback and Firebaugh native Josh Allen dines at Wool Growers when he visits family in the off season. He's flanked here by owners Ruth Reynosa and Talisa Vander Poel. Photo: Wool Growers Restaurant Facebook page.

When he's not throwing touchdowns, or scrambling to beat a defender who has a mind to tackle him, *Buffalo Bills* quarterback Josh Allen thinks about his hometown on a California back road in the Central Valley.

Josh does not get back to the Valley often, but when he does, he makes plans to eat at *Wool Growers* in Los Banos.

"He usually comes by in the weeks after the Super Bowl," co-owner Ruth Reynosa says. She runs the restaurant with her daughter Talisa.

That appreciation of the family atmosphere of *Wool Growers* seems to have been passed on to a new generation of NFL greats. That's probably why Josh Allen, a native of nearby Firebaugh in Fresno County, enjoys eating there when he's in the area visiting family.

"He likes our lamb stew and the last time he was here a few months ago he had a New York strip steak."

The *Wool Growers Restaurant* began in late 1800s. Specialties include roast lamb, pork chops, and baked chicken. It is also known for a lamb stew that customers have enjoyed for years.
Basque country straddles the border of Spain and France. Many of the Basque people raised sheep and have been coming to California for over a century.

"Running a restaurant is not easy," Ruth says. "Running it together with my daughter is much better this way as you need to trust your business partner." Daughter Talisa Vander Poel agrees. "This place is set up family style, our customers are like family, so it makes sense that a family runs it."

Wool Growers had another loyal customer who was known for his appreciation of good food and excellent hospitality. The late John Madden was a loyal customer, and during his active years, he'd visit the place often.

The coach and television personality who died in December 2021, loved eating at the *Wool Growers*. Known for his hundreds of thousands of miles logged on the road in his custom-made bus (he hated airplanes), Madden had a lust for life both as a Super Bowl winning coach and an Emmy winning sports analyst.

He also had an appreciation for food, and had favorite restaurants all around the United States. Travelling from city to city to cover football games gave him an exposure to where some of the best places to eat were in practically every region of the nation.

But his home base was the Bay Area, and one of his favorite places to eat was *Wool Growers*.

"I hear people talking about him eating here," says Ruth who took over the restaurant a few years ago. "He was a customer before we started here."

While there are apparently no pictures of John Madden dining at the restaurant, Ruth shared one photo that was on *Reddit.com* showing what appears to be the back of his head wearing a *Wool Growers* hat. There's also a reference of his affection for the place in a Sports Illustrated profile.

Wool Growers Restaurant at 609 H Street in Los Banos, California. Photo: Wool Growers Facebook Page

Ruth says many people observed him at the restaurant on several occasions. "One customer who remembers him eating here told us he enjoyed the ambience of the place,"

Ruth and Talisa are happy their restaurant touched John Madden enough for him to keep coming back year after year.

Now with Josh Allen making *Wool Growers* a regular stop when he visits during the off season, both owners hope to see more of him in the coming years.

They hope all their customers feel the same way.

Branding Memories
At the Branding Iron

The iconic neon sign for the Branding Iron Restaurant on 16th Street in Merced. Photo: Steve Newvine

"Let's meet somewhere in-between," the voice on the other end of the phone suggested. "How about the *Branding Iron* in Merced?"

That voice from nearly twenty years ago was from the head of development for a national charity's regional office. He was setting up an appointment to meet me and to talk about a position the organization was looking to fill.

The year was 2006. It was the first time I would drive from my home in Fresno to the City of Merced. It would not be the last time.

I had never heard of the *Branding Iron*. But upon entering the restaurant, it was clear to me this place *was the meeting place* for Merced.

The job I drove fifty miles north to discuss was never offered. But it was nice to see the inside of an authentic California steakhouse.

The *Branding Iron* changed hands a few years ago. Now a new generation has assumed stewardship over this beloved local dining landmark. The owners advertise that all profits from the restaurant will be going to local charitable causes.

From the dark wood grain walls, to the cattle branding motif throughout the restaurant, the *Branding Iron* was a perfect meeting place for business settings, service club meetings, or a special night out.

Two months after my first visit to the Sixteenth Street establishment back in 2006, I got another call from another organization. After discussing the job, I was asked to come up to Merced again. "We'll have lunch at the *Branding Iron*," this new voice declared.

This time around, the outcome of the business discussed proved positive for me. The lunch led to another meeting, and eventually to an offer to work in Merced.

The rest is history as my wife and I settled in, bought a house, got involved, and made this community our new hometown.

Through it all, the *Branding Iron* was part of my Merced experience. The Rotary Club I joined met there every week. Other groups would have meetings in one of the banquet rooms there.

My first office was next door at an old railroad station. The restaurant owner would frequently stop in to use the copy machine. My organization would hold special meetings there.

Unique features of the Branding Iron are the branding symbols seen throughout the restaurant. Photo: Steve Newvine

I recall one afternoon when then Governor Schwarzenegger spoke at a luncheon held at the County Fairgrounds. After the Governor left town, I got a call from one of the field assistants of an elected member of the legislature. That person asked whether I could join other field assistants for a late afternoon happy hour at the *Branding Iron*. I joined the group briefly after work and I enjoyed connecting with this circle of professionals.

Most of my business lunches were held there not only for the convenient walk to and from the office, but also for the statement the restaurant made about Merced. That statement in my mind is this: we are a friendly place, most of the people here are honest to the core, you'll be treated well and you will want to stay here for the rest of your life.

Remember that if you do go, beef is king.

32,000 Girl Scout Cookies

Volunteers loading their cars and SUVs with all varieties of Girl Scout cookies. Photo: Steve Newvine

It was a great philosopher, my wife, who once said, "God made cookies so that kids would drink their milk."

She was right. There's a special time each year when Girl Scouts and their leaders deliver pre-sale orders and conduct cash sales in front of selected locations.

On a springtime weekday morning, Merced County Girl Scout leaders took delivery of hundreds of cases filled with all varieties of the iconic treats. They were all there: *Thin Mints, Adventurefuls, Lemonades, Trefoils,* and many others.

One savvy Scout leader did some quick calculations on her phone calculator app and put the actual number of cookies coming into the pick-up location at just under thirty-two thousand.

Laurie is the senior coordinator for cookie sales in her community. "This is one activity they look forward to every year," she says.

Girl Scout cookies are an icon of the organization. The annual sales activity raises money for individual troops, and provides soft-skill training such as dealing with people and business ethics. Photo: Steve Newvine

"They can choose to put the cookie sale profits into a variety of initiatives," another scout leader said. "We have a flora and fauna project, a vernal pools study, World Thinking Day and we even bought masks for first responders."

One local group prioritized a local museum with their cookie proceeds. "The Girl Scouts bought part of a new fence at the museum," the scout leader said.

Adult leaders helping the Girl Scouts do a little bit of everything. Some organize group projects, others chaperone camp outings. Still others take time to pick up boxes of cookies in the family SUV.

One mom was pretty proud of her ability to stow away case after case of *Peanut Butter Patties, Caramel deLites*, and even a gluten-free selection among other varieties. "I didn't realize I had that much space in there," she said.

TOP 5 GIRL SCOUT COOKIES IN MERCED COUNTY
(based on orders by the local troops)
1. *Thin Mints*
2. *Caramel deLites*
3. *Peanut Butter Patties*
4. *Lemonades*
5. *Adventurefuls*

As with so many things in life, it is not just about the cookies. The Scout website states that cookie sales teach goal setting, decision making, money management, people skills, and business ethics.

It's good for the customer as well. Buying Girl Scout cookies helps these young entrepreneurs hone in on each of the goals.

Plus, the cookies may even get adults to drink their milk.

Say Cheese in Hilmar

Hilmar Cheese Visitor Center in Hilmar, Merced County. Photo: Steve Newvine

In case I haven't mentioned it in at least half the dozen-plus books I've written over the years, I grew up in a small town upstate New York. It was farm country, and in northern New York State, that meant it was dairy country.

Growing up in dairy country in upstate New York, a grade school class trip to a milk processing plant was always a possibility for me.

Some things never change. Whether it's 1968 when I was in grade school, or fifty-five years later in Hilmar, California.

On any given school day, it is not uncommon to find a busload of school children taking the tour of Hilmar Cheese in northern Merced County. The company's visitor center is a hit for school groups who want something close to the home, full of interesting things to see, and that ends with ice cream.

On a breezy morning in early spring, grade schoolers from Ceres Unified School District in adjacent Stanislaus County, their teachers and several parent chaperones took the free tour at Hilmar Cheese. The easiest way to get there is to head west for five miles at the Lander Road exit from highway 99.

"They love it here," one of the Hilmar Cheese gift shop employees said as a customer acknowledged the large crowd of youngsters.

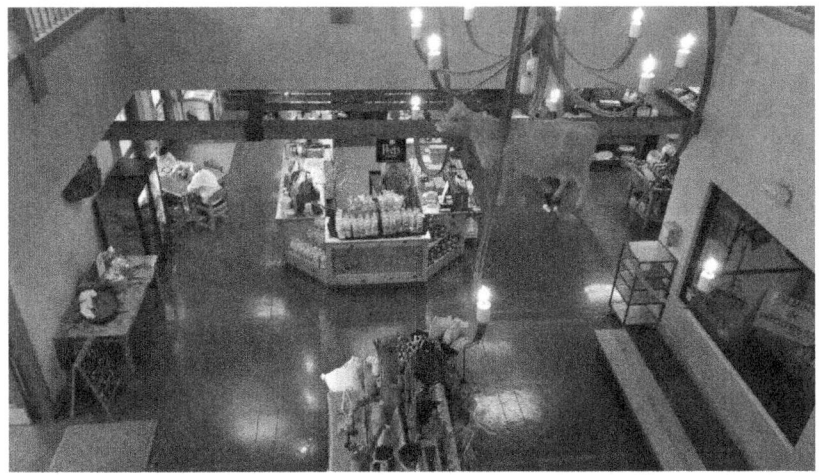

The view overhead looking down on the Hilmar Cheese Visitor Center Gift Shop and Café. Photo: Steve Newvine

Hilmar Cheese has been around since 1984 when eleven dairy farms banded together with an idea scribbled on a napkin at a coffee shop.

The company's story actually begins at the turn of the twentieth century. That's when many dairy farmers settled in Hilmar to make a living milking cows and selling their dairy products.

Jersey cows produced so-called high solids milk. By the eighties, that group of farmers formed the company to maximize opportunities for other farmers by seeking out fair prices for the milk produced.

The company prides itself on strong customer relationships and assuring that their milk brand unlocks the full nutritional and economic value it holds.

The model must work, as the company is now in the hands of the second and third generations of many of the original founders.

While the company also operates a cheese making facility in Texas, the home base is secure in the rural surroundings of the Central Valley of California.

The Visitor Center honors that humble beginning with displays showing how the company has grown over the past four decades.

The Center welcomes children and others just about any day of the year with the exception of the major holidays. The tour is free, and ends at the gift shop and café where cheese products and sandwiches are available for a cost comparable to what you might pay at a grocery store or diner.

There's also an outdoor waterfall with a walking path to give visitors a chance to walk off any extra calories from lunch at the café.

The company says twenty-percent of all the cheese sold in the US comes from Hilmar Cheese. In many cases, the cheese is sold under a different brand name. Cheese from Hilmar Cheese is sold in over fifty countries.

In most of the tours given by the team at Hilmar Cheese, visitors learn how cheese is made with hands-on exhibits about cows and the dairy industry. They can see workers packaging large crates of cheese.

On this particular morning in May, the children were involved in a game that simulated the ice cream making process. The youngsters were wide-eyed and anxious about the game.

That might have been the result of a subtle promise by the group leader of real ice cream for everyone at the end of the tour.

A giant mural on the side of one of the buildings at Hilmar Cheese. Photo: Steve Newvine

Children enjoy class trips like this one at Hilmar Cheese. But clearly the free tour in a clean and air-conditioned visitor center makes for an easy event pod for people of any age. Add to this a better understanding of the role of dairy farmers in a region that relies heavily on agricultural producers for jobs and economic activity.

All the way around, the tour is a win.

Cars, Balloons & Electric Planes

Cars & Coffee Monthly Shows

Tom and Emily Bustos along with their classic automobiles: a Maserati Granturismo & a Porsche 911. Photo: Steve Newvine

California life can be defined by many with a question about the kind of car one drives.

Most folks will tell you they drive a *Hyundai Elantra* because it gets good gas mileage. Others will say they prefer their *Toyota Rav 4* because it is easy to carry stuff from the grocery store or the home center.

In California, it seems every community has a car story. Some of the most interesting stories are about the older cars better known as the classics.

You'll see these classics at car shows that seem to take place somewhere in the state practically every weekend.

Tom Bustos remembers the day a car show provided a once-in-lifetime experience for a woman. Back in 2022, a family cleaned up an old Dodge Dart that was exactly like the one their mom had back in her youth. The family surprised the mom by taking her to the *Cars and Coffee* show.

"They made sure the car was there before she arrived, Tom recalls. "She had no idea that this car was going to be part of their family that day. It was a joy to watch that reveal unfold."

This Oldsmobile is one of many classics on display at the monthly Cars and Coffee Merced (California) show held on the first Saturday of each month from March through October at the Merced Mall north parking lot. Photo: Steve Newvine

Personal stories like these keep Tom and his wife Emily inspired to stage the monthly car show in the north parking lot at Merced Mall in the Central Valley.

Cars and Coffee started when Emily and Tom thought the time was right for a car show that was free, family friendly, and not too narrow in focus.

"There were a lot of shows, but they were very specific about car types or time periods," Emily said. "We wanted a venue that was open to everyone, and any kind of car."

From that basic concept emerged *Cars and Coffee.* The property manager at Merced Mall offered the north parking area for displays, Merced Car Wash emerged as a partner to hold the events, and Jantz Bakery offered to provide morning coffee.

The couple use social media to let people know about upcoming car shows. Word-of-mouth has also helped spread the word.

On the first Saturday of every month beginning in March, *Cars and Coffee* welcomes the cars, their owners, and the public for a few hours of nostalgia, reconnection, and car talk.

"We've been hosting Cars and Coffee in Merced since 2016," said Tom Bustos. "We feel really blessed."

The monthly activity provides all of the good things a car show can create and it helps community organizations along the way. The July event raises money for the *Carlos Viera Foundation Race for Autism*.

Other groups that benefit from the showcase of vintage cars include Cub Scout Pack 96 when the annual Pinewood Derby is staged on site alongside the automobile displays. "That event includes a scavenger hunt where participants find cars with particular histories," Tom said.

There are a lot of classic car enthusiasts in the Central Valley of California. This monthly event provides the family friendly venue where everyone is welcome and any car can be displayed. The Bustos get into the act with their two cars. One drives a *Maserati* and the other drives a *Porsche*.

The other added bonus of *Cars and Coffee Merced* is the creation of new memories connecting people to a special set of wheels in their lives.

One car enthusiast shared a story about selling a classic car at a reduced price to a terminally ill friend so that the friend could enjoy it in what would be his final days.

Others can recall a specific type of car that was exactly like the car a close relative had back decades ago.

Still others just get a kick out of seeing all the cars

A classic Ford Thunderbird brightens the scenery at Cars and Coffee Merced. Photo: Steve Newvine

Cars and Coffee is held every first Saturday morning from March through October in the north parking area at Merced Mall. There is no entry fee for cars and no admission charge to the public. A raffle helps generate enough money to provide some light snacks, pay for the event insurance, and purchase additional prizes.

The purpose is quite simple according to Tom: "The goal is just to bring motor enthusiasts of all kinds together." Memories continue to be made month after month, wheel after wheel.

Modesto-Car Town

This convertible is one of many vintage cars that will be on display when the Graffiti USA Classic Car Museum opens in 2024 or 2025. Photo: Steve Newvine

When the conversation turns to classic cars in California, a lot of attention is being paid to Modesto in the Central Valley about an hour south of Sacramento.

In Modesto, a young boy's 1950s dreams of hot rods, cruising down the main drag in town, and maybe some unauthorized pranks fueled an imagination that would be forever memorized in the movie *American Graffitti*.

George Lucas made the film, and helped usher in an era of nostalgia for the fifties and sixties. He grew up in Modesto and his recollections of life as a teen in the years before Vietnam and political assassinations are now forever preserved.

He was also the creative force behind the *Star Wars* movies. While he would visit Modesto on occasion, he really left it behind choosing the Bay Area to build a museum to celebrate the *Star Wars* phenomenon.

The City paid tribute to Lucas with a bronze interpretation of a scene from *American Graffitti*. The bronze shows anxious teens fawning over a classic automobile.

Now the Modesto car guys from the fifties and sixties are the seniors with memories of that era. Some have taken up the charge to put the community's car story into proper context.

As a young adult in Modesto in the 1950s and early sixties, John Sanders loved working on cars. He and his buddies liked showing off their hot rods on Tenth and Eleventh Streets in the city. "I fixed up a 1960 Aston Martin DB4," Don laughs. "And my wife and I took it on our honeymoon."

That love of fixing up and showing off classic cars is what propelled Don and some of his fellow business owners to help start a museum along Ninth Street in the city.

The Graffiti USA Classic Car Museum celebrates the heritage of classic cars as depicted in the iconic movie *American Graffiti*.

The Graffiti USA Classic Car Museum showcases vintage automobiles. Photo: Steve Newvine

A non-profit corporation was formed a few years ago to take the idea of a showcase for cars and the Modesto way of life during the *American Graffiti* era and turn it into a museum.

Over a million dollars in monetary and non-monetary donations have been received. The museum will get a local government grant for another million dollars over the next few years while more fundraising continues.

The corporation has purchased two former seed and grain warehouses and has been working to get the museum showroom ready for an opening that is now expected to happen in 2024 or 2025.

"The costs of making our building legal and a great car museum have been huge," John says. "We're building the museum constantly, but it is at the speed of donations."

The buildings have over forty-thousand square feet for museum displays, a banquet hall, and office space. Visitors see an impressive collection of vintage automobiles upon entering the building. The main display area starts with a large mural showing the Modesto arch with a classic 1960s era convertible.

Beyond the classic car collection, phase two is planned as a re-creation of the downtown area as it was back in the heyday of the cruising era of the fifties and sixties.

The *Modesto Radio Museum* hopes to occupy a spot in that section to salute local radio stations such as KBEE, better known at that time as *the Bee*. *The Bee* played the rock-and-roll hits that might have been blaring on the AM radios in the cars cruising down Tenth and Eleventh Streets. The Radio Museum currently lives on-line (ModestoRadioMuseum.org)

"*The Graffiti USA Classic Car Museum* will celebrate cars, but it will also celebrate Modesto as it was back in the era of *American Graffiti*," John says.

Architectural sketches for the museum pay homage to the drive-in burger joint style popularized in the movie as well as television programs like *Happy Days*.

The museum site along Ninth Street connects to another big part of regional history. Ninth Street was part of the old highway 99 that remains following the construction of the highway 99 that moves traffic south to Fresno, north to Sacramento, and west to the connector routes that lead to the San Francisco Bay area

That historic link to highway 99 is part of an effort to locate a California Rest Area at the site of the museum. There's a lot more work that needs to be done before that idea can come to fruition, but the museum leadership is encouraged with the progress made to date.

In fact, there's a lot to be proud of as the museum looks back on the effort to acquire the two buildings, oversee the preparation of the display space for the first phase, and looking ahead to a grand opening in the near future.

The vision to celebrate Modesto's car cruising history clouded over for a while when the pandemic hit in 2020. "COVID just slowed things down," John says. "But we are looking ahead."

Fundraising will continue to be the primary focus as the museum moves forward. The gift shop opened ahead of the museum and sold tee-shirts, post cards, even bottles of a specially labeled bottle of wine. All profits go to the museum.

The museum also obtained a California business license to allow for selling cars as a way to raise funds for the effort. They are selling cars and accepting qualified vehicles for donation to the museum. While it may sound a little unusual for a car museum to be in the car business, this group is actually borrowing the idea from another organization doing the same thing.

The group has reached out to native son George Lucas as well as to former *Tonight Show* host Jay Leno for support and encouragement.

In the meantime, car guys like John Sanders will continue to pour more time and sweat equity into the project. Not all his time though. He's currently working on restoring another car. To paraphrase an often used saying, you can take the man out of his car, but you cannot take the car out of the man.

(Top) An artist rendering of what the Graffiti USA Classic Car Museum might look like in a few years. (Bottom) The Museum main entrance.

Let's Go Fly a Kite

These larger than life kites entertain residents on a windy springtime afternoon   Photo-Steve Newvine

It was a site normally seen on a coastal beach in California. Only this time, the spectacle was taking place in an inland city park for the entertainment of local residents.

Up close on the park grounds, the sight was nothing short of spectacular.

These are the kites Mike Macias and his brother Rob spend their free time putting up in sky on a windy day. Mike started the pastime several years ago as a diversion from his regular job as a truck driver.

"A week behind the wheel is enough," he says of his handling of an eighteen-wheeler on a California expressway. "On a weekend, I look for a place to put up our kites.

A shark kite lurks over the playground as the Macias brothers entertain families. Photo: Steve Newvine

Mike goes big when he flies his super-sized kites. Some measure more than two-hundred feet from top to bottom, based on my own estimates. All are powered by wind, and the steady hands of both pilots.

"My brother and I love putting them up, and keeping them airborne," he says.

The kites were a popular attraction at local events such as the Livingston Kite Festival that was held every spring until

2019. The festival was cancelled in 2020 and 2021 as a COVID precaution.

Mike & Rob Macias steady a big kite. Photo: Steve Newvine

Kite flying gets people outdoors and has social distancing practically built in. Each kite flyer needs a lot of space to do the work that has to be done.

"We used to go all over the state," Mike says. "Everyone likes to see these kites up in the air."

The brothers anchor the kites to trees and/or posts depending on the venue. The wind keeps them up for as long as Mother Nature will allow.

There were lawn chairs out in the open space, children on the playground equipment, and lots of heads looking upward.

In the meantime, Mike and Rob will continue to look for a warm, breezy afternoon and take their kites out of the storage cases. The fun continues.

They are two brothers seeking out ways to bring joy to families through these spectacular kites.

Wings Up on Electric Airplanes-

The four Pipistrel Alpha Trainers on display at Fresno Chandler Executive Airport. Photo: New Vision Aviation

Imagine a time when most airplanes will run off power cells that recharge in the same way electric cars do today.

All-electric aircraft are already in use in the Central Valley of California as part of a demonstration project.

The non-profit group New Vision Aviation facilitated the creation of an eight-county coalition of local governments to apply for a federal grant that has effectively jump-started the concept.

The original idea came to Joseph Oldham, the former Sustainability Manager for the City of Fresno and former

Executive Director of a transportation planning non-profit. His accomplishments include nurturing relationships between businesses and the government to get zero-emission buses into public transit fleets.

He reached out to the manager of the Fresno Chandler Executive Airport to brainstorm a plan to buy four experimental electric airplanes from a Slovenia company. The planes are manufactured in Italy.

Joseph did a lot of leg work in preparing the application for a grant to demonstrate advanced transportation technology. He believes the planes, along with charging stations at airports within range, will do just that.

After presenting the idea to local governments, writing a grant proposal and pushing the initiative forward, New Vision Aviation was successful.

The idea boils down to creating a network of chargers at local municipal airports such as Merced Municipal Airport and Castle Airport in Atwater. The experimental aircraft has a two-hour flying range, so the need for a charging network is critical to the success of the program.

One of the four Pipistrel Alpha Trainers at the Fresno Chandler Airport getting recharged. Photo: New Vision Aviation.

Four two-seater planes, known as the Pipistrel Alpha Trainer, were purchased and are in use right now.

Joseph has been a pilot for over forty years and has been a passionate advocate for sustainable transportation throughout those years. He says this concept could create the next era of aviation. "With chargers at these municipal airports, the San Joaquin Valley could support the operation of small all-electric aircraft," he says.

Alongside the track of creating a network of planes and charging stations to support all-electric aircraft, New Vision Aviation is developing a second track: getting high school and college-aged men and women excited about careers in aviation. Reduced maintenance and lower electric (as opposed to fossil fuel) costs create an opportunity to bring more diversity into aviation.

The New Vision website envisions a mentorship program where pilots become mentors for young people interested in aviation. "We've worked with Boeing on identifying the need to increase interest among younger people in flying," he says.

All-electric aircraft offers the opportunity to lower the cost of flying when compared to conventional small airplanes. Some in the industry estimate an hour of flying time now runs a student about $200. This is due primarily to the higher cost of fuel. With an all-electric aircraft, some observers believe that cost could be cut by half or more.

Joseph mentors a young student interested in aviation right now. That student is learning to operate small aircraft. The student, his flight trainer, and Joseph were featured in a recent episode of the PBS series *NOVA*. The segment was titled *The All-Electric Airplane Race*.

Joseph flew one of the Pipistrel Alpha Trainers to Sacramento in the summer of 2021. The one-hundred, fifty mile demonstration flight, with recharging stops to show

how the concept would work, was labeled a success. "We want to raise awareness of the potential of an all-electric fleet and charging stations throughout California and eventually throughout the nation."

Now that the initial grant has been approved, New Vision is awaiting F.A.A. approval to start a flight school with the planes. Achieving that goal may be out on the time horizon, but the initiative to bring more young people into the world of aviation will continue to move forward.

It may not be too far into the future when a young Californian teen can connect with a pilot mentor to help learn more about the discipline and rewards from flying as a career.

The relatively brief history of aviation has two revolutions so far.

The first revolution was powered flight. The second was the introduction of jets. Electric propulsion is the third revolution. This entire effort is about making the most of the third revolution and making it more than just an alternative way to fly.

++

Agriculture

Nuts Have a Fighting Chance

Springtime blossoms on an orchard in Stanislaus County. Photo: Steve Newvine

Driving through California's back roads can offer sites of incredible agricultural bounty. In the spring, many communities sponsor Blossom Trails where folks can drive using specially marked maps to see the floral that comes in advance of the primary growing season.

In the summer, look for the green as irrigation delivers water to orchards and vineyards. Steady sunshine day after day adds the right combination to make Central California the world's leader in agricultural production of fruits and vegetables.

Then autumn arrives and with it the harvest season. Grape harvesters grab the fruit from the vines at just the right sweetness as measured by the grower. Brown paper lines many fields of grapes that will dry out and become raisins.

Heavy duty farm equipment shakes the nuts from almond and other nut orchards. With the strategic timing of the harvest comes the annual worry as to what growers can expect from the market in any particular year.

It seems that every year becomes one of the most challenging growing seasons for nut growers throughout the Central Valley of California.

"This is a difficult year for almond growers and the whole industry", a spokesman for the Almond Board of California said. "Costs are up and prices have been down, while shipping issues and problems throughout the supply chain have added to the complexities of being a farmer."

The challenge is so real, the US Department of Agriculture estimates the 2021 almond crop was down eleven percent from 2021. That estimate is seven percent down from their forecast at the beginning of the growing season in May.

Inflation is one of the three top challenges for growers in the Central Valley. Fuel costs are considered by many to be a stand-alone issue as it permeates a grower's entire operation.

"Almond growers are putting what resources they can afford this year into producing their crop, and their efforts show," the Almond Board spokesman said.

The President of the Merced County Farm Bureau agrees. Joe Sansoni says inflation has really hit all growers hard. "For example, repair parts for equipment have doubled and in some cases tripled in cost, and often are backordered or simply unavailable," Joe said. "This goes for every single category including labor."

A lot of growers switched to growing almonds in recent years due to the higher return of investment the crop provided in the 2010s. Those margins have taken a hit in recent years, but most growers expected some retraction as more crops were being produced.

A water pump set up near an almond orchard as growers look for enough to complete the crop. Photo: Steve Newvine

Availability of water also concerned growers in 2020s. According to the Farm Bureau's Joe Sansoni, the challenges varied depending on where a grower is located and whether or not they had access to wells and/or surface water (supplied by an irrigation district).

"Growers with both wells and surface water in most parts of Merced County had enough water to grow a full crop," Joe said. "Some growers were forced to dry up and remove lower yielding fields to divert the water they had to younger, more productive blocks, or in some cases to other higher-paying crops."

With the value add from creative retailers, nuts are on display at the annual Nut Festival held at the Merced Fairgrounds. Photo: Steve Newvine

In the City of Merced, the annual Nut Festival is held in October at the County Fairgrounds. This event is designed to celebrate the contributions of nut growers to the quality of life in the Central Valley. More than four-thousand people attended in 2022.

Central Valley agriculture can still hold on to the promise that almonds, walnuts and pistachios will continue to be major crops in the near future.

Two things are certain when it comes to the local nut harvest. One is that a festival such as the one held in Merced will continue to celebrate the successes of the crop that generates an estimated half billion dollars according to the Merced County Agriculture Commissioner annual report.

The other certainty is that growers will continue to work through the challenges of previous years with optimism for next season.

The Almond Board of California is optimistic for Central Valley growers saying than in spite of the road blocks, the 2022 crop in California was among the largest on record. The spokesman for Board says, "It reflects the efforts of growers to meet the high global demand for a steady supply of high quality California almonds".

Bees are Working Toward a Better Harvest

Bee hives can be seen near dozens of orchards throughout the Central Valley. Photo: Steve Newvine

It's a sight that is almost as welcome a sign of spring as the blossoms on an almond tree. Every spring, bee hives are placed at many agricultural enterprises throughout California's Central Valley.

The bees are pollinating the blossoms.

The bees feed off and transport pollen grains as they move throughout an orchard. Quite simply, the success of the crop yield is directly related to the success of the bees.

Greg Shved knows how important this link between bees and crop yield can be. He is a commercial beekeeper who is grateful this year's bee season is winding down successfully.

"Bee populations are definitely still threatened," Greg says. "The biggest issues are diseases within the honey bees themselves that are getting harder to treat year to year."

Greg is part of Exchange Bees, a supplier of honey bees for almond growers in California.

Honey bees are a key component to a successful yield. Photo: Steve Newvine

Bees are not the only pollinators. According to the Pollinator Partnership, a non-profit group that sets out to protect and grow the bee population, bats, beetles, birds, butterflies, flies, moths and a few small mammals are also part of the mix of pollinators.

But all experts agree, bees are the largest category of pollinators for agriculture production.

Greg adds, "The bee season for spring pollination comes to an end in mid-March. There are other seasons with lower demand throughout the year."

The Pollinator Partnership states that one out of every three bites of food we consume comes from a source that needs pollination. That's why any threat to bee populations is taken seriously.

"We're able to treat diseases that impact bees with pollination money," Greg says.

The Pollinator Partnership, also known as P2, points to relationships with research scientists developed over thirty years ago to study bees.

Conservation strategies have been implemented, and many partners are making the effort to secure and grow the bee population.

In 2020, there was concern over the so-called murder hornets. These hornets made their way to the US by way of Asia, being discovered first in the state of Washington and later in Canada.

According to a report from the Weather Channel, the hornets pose a threat. With avenom that can kill in high doses, these hornets can be a threat.

A typical hive of honey bees could be destroyed by these murder hornets in just a few hours. The hornets eat the heads off of honey bees and take over the hives. That's a scary thought for honey bees, growers, and the general population.

According to Greg, so far, California orchards have been free of this threat.

For now, many growers are hoping for the best in terms of keeping bee populations healthy and their crop yields rising.

They will only know how successful the season will be as harvesting and processing resumes later in the year.

If all goes well, we can expect the cycle to resume again next year when the bees return to the orchards throughout California.

Soon the hives will be taken away from this orchard in the Central Valley and the next stage of the growing cycle will move forward. Photo: Steve Newvine

Harvest Time

(left) An orchard of oranges in Madera County, and (right) a cotton harvester is working the fields in Fresno County. Photos by Steve Newvine

Pick just about any month, any time of year, and chances are there's a crop about to be harvested by a grower in California.

Most of the bounty will be found off the beaten paths of this state where agriculture ranks near or at the top among all industry.

Depending on which source is looked up on-line, you can learn how ag generated over fifty-billion dollars in cash receipts in 2021 (University of Arkansas System Division of Ag.), that the state is the largest producer and exporter of dairy products, fruits and nuts in the nation (Business.ca.gov>industries> agriculture), and how ag tops the film industry and service sector including tourism in terms of economic impact (worldatlas.com>articles>what are the big industries in California).

But to the central question about what you see out your car window when you travel the back roads of California, *why is ag more successful here than in other states?* That's another question that may get you different answers depending on who you talk to or where you search on the internet.

Most agree that the soil created by the erosion from the mountains many thousands of years ago deposited rich sediments that created excellent topsoil (farmtogether.com>learn blog>why-california). Many concur the climate is considered a Mediterranean climate where, when properly irrigated, more than four-hundred commodities flourish.

(left) Cherries are one of the first crops to yield in the spring months. These were found at a "u-pick" orchard in northern Merced County). (right) Watermelon, or at least the first planting of watermelon, begins harvesting generally in June or July with a second planting ready to harvest later in the summer. This group of watermelon pickers were using a tried-and-true "cut, pitch and place into the bin" method at a field in Atwater, Merced County. The website SeeCalifornia.com, states that growers in the state produce approximately three-hundred and thirty tons of watermelon annually. Photo: Steve Newvine

Some sources will put information and technology ahead of agriculture in the ranking of industries of the state. The information and technology field is constantly creating new products. Banking and finance also appears on many ranking lists (elevenrecruiting.com>top-industries-in-california).

But agriculture continues to grow in terms of total cash receipts as well as the continued increases in the value of farmland.

You need to look no further than the chapter in this book about the nut crop to read about the threats to agriculture. Every industry has a share of strengths, weaknesses, opportunities and threats. The so-called SWOT (strengths, weaknesses, opportunities and threats) analysis is a foundational tenet of most business survival strategies.

Grapes are laid out to dry in the warmth of the California sun as they become raisins. This particular crop was found near highway 145 in eastern Fresno County. Photo: Steve Newvine

The tug between growers and buyers is as much a part of agriculture as the annual miracle of putting seed into the ground or preparing orchards for the next growing season. Those fields produce the greatest farm bounty in the world. We can see it right in front of our eyes along the back roads of California.

See you at the World Ag Expo

Major farm equipment have massive displays of their tractors and other implements at the World Ag Expo, Tulare, California. Photo: Steve Newvine

For over fifty years, agricultural producers from all over the United States have been coming to the World Ag Expo in the heart of the California's Central Valley in Tulare.

The Expo is a showcase of the latest in farm equipment, the newest technology to help growers, and a social event bringing farmers together in a positive environment.

The *World Ag Expo* is produced by the *International Agri-Center*, a non-profit organization dedicated to farm education and agriculture promotion. What started in 1968 as a farm show on seventy acres has expanded over the years.

Ag producers in the tens of thousands come to the World Ag Expo to see the latest farm equipment and technology. Photo: Steve Newvine

The *International Agri-Center* has grown to over seven-hundred acres. The Agri-Center, Expo site, and parking lots use up about forty-percent of the total acreage. The rest is farmland where some of the Valley's signature crops such as almonds, cotton, and hay are raised.

Just before the pandemic hit, over one-hundred thousand people attended the Expo. The event was on-line due to COVID restrictions in 2021.

There are nearly fifteen-hundred exhibitors showing off the latest in farm equipment, agriculture products, and business technology available to this segment of the economy.

An estimated thirty-plus area non-profit organizations use the event as a fund-raising opportunity by selling food to hungry Expo visitors.

"Tulare is a close-knit community," one of the volunteers said. "We have a legacy of giving back and this Expo has a tradition of giving back by letting groups raise money for their causes."

Over twelve-hundred volunteers are recruited to help with all kinds of duties such as directing parking, troubleshooting technical issues with vendors, and assisting attendees.

The *International Agri-Center* is led by an all-volunteer board of directors, a full-time staff, and more than twelve hundred volunteers who offer their time to work the Expo.

Without the volunteers, most of what happens during these early February days at the Expo would simply not be possible.

The regional economy benefits from the deluge of visitors to the *World Ag Expo*. Local hotels fill up, area dining establishments are busy, and other retail cash registers are ringing.

But more important to the economy is the activity among the vendors who connect with area agricultural producers to provide information on the latest equipment, software technology, and new ideas.

"We did an economic impact study on the event in 2020," Jennifer Fawkes said. "*World Ag Expo* had a fifty-two million dollar impact on California two years ago."

That economic impact study measured hotel room nights, restaurant attendance, and miscellaneous retail among the attendees and vendors connected with the Expo. Ag sales between vendors and farmers were not measured.

But the vendors attest to the value of meeting their customers face to face to explain the latest in equipment, technology, and products.

"What's important to us is making that face-to-face connection with the customer," says Sheldon Litwiller of *Litwiller Fabrication*, an ag building solutions company. "A sale may come later, but for us the purpose of the show is to let the customer know how we can help them."

Most of the vendors here agree there's nothing quite like an in-person trade show to connect sellers to buyers.

Trade shows get customers into an environment with similar business operators.

Vendors can establish a rapport with a customer from a brief greeting as they pass by a display booth. Questions may get answered. Trust begins to build.

"Our customers are important," says Matt Daley of Waikato Milking Systems, an automation solutions company for dairies. "But equally important is our company's support of the distributors and retailers who work with the customers."

Matt concedes there may be more cost effective ways to support their distributor and retailing network, but showing up for this show, one of the biggest farm shows in the world, makes good sense for the company. "This is our way to say thanks to them as well," he says.

So whether it's the big equipment manufacturers who want the large exposition space, the non-profit organizations that earn a big portion of their annual budgets, or the farmer and his family coming out to meet other farmers, the tradition continues in Tulare County.

Author note. You can hear the author discuss the World Ag Expo in a radio interview with KYOS-AM in Merced, California by going to YouTube.com and entering "Steve Newvine World Ag Expo" in the search feature. The interview runs about eight minutes.

Community Service

Service Clubs Give Back

The founding members of the Merced Council of the Knights of Columbus. The local Council was chartered in 1922. Photo: St. Teresa of Calcutta Council, Knights of Columbus

On just about any weekend in practically every community throughout California, a service club is hosting some kind of event to raise money for charity.

Whether it's a dinner, farm festival, rummage sale, or a myriad of other activities, communities have come to depend on service clubs as well as other non-profit organizations to pull all the details together and pull off a successful event.

Put yourself into the year 1922 for a few moments and think about the men pictured in the black and white photograph at the beginning of this chapter.

They were the founding members of what was first called the Merced Council of the Knights of Columbus, a service club of Catholic men.

The Knights were started in 1882 by a Connecticut priest as a means for Catholic men to work together so as to help others and display patriotism.

From that humble start some one-hundred forty years ago, chapters of the Knights formed all over the country.

The Knights founding principles are charity, unity, fraternity, and patriotism. There are nearly two-million Knights throughout the world. In 1922, the *Merced Council* was chartered.

Longtime member Randy Starkweather says the local organization changed its name from the *Merced Council* to the *St. Teresa of Calcutta* Council around the time Mother Teresa was canonized as a saint in September of 2016. The world-famous missionary died in 1997 and the canonization process began right away.

Locally, the Council provides support to the Alpha Crisis Center in Merced as well as a faith-based nonprofit organization known as Possibility Productions. Local

Knights also help seminarians as they study for pastoral roles in the church. They provide service for a number of initiatives and organizations within the St. Patrick's community.

Knights are called upon to provide the extra hands on just about any church project. They pride themselves are being able to mobilize to help out within a moment's notice.

The Merced Council of the Knights of Columbus changed its name to the St. Teresa of Calcutta Council to honor the missionary nun Mother Teresa upon her canonization in 2016.

In the years leading up to the Merced group's founding, the Knights worldwide raised money and provided so-called "K of C" huts throughout Europe during World War I. The huts were rest and recreational facilities that offered social services to Allied servicemen of all faiths.

The huts sprung up throughout the United States and Europe providing religious services, supplies, and recreation under the motto, "Everybody Welcome, Everything Free."

This effort led to the eventual development in World War II of the non-profit group known as the USO (United Service Organization).

Following World War II, Knights all over America lobbied for public adoption of the words "under God" in the *Pledge of Allegiance*.

Those words were officially added to the Pledge following the signing of a bill into law by President Eisenhower in 1953.

"We have the Knights to thank for those two words," said Randy.

While the international organization marked a 140th anniversary, the Merced, California fraternal group celebrated a century of service in 2022. As the St. Teresa of Calcutta Council of the Knights of Columbus begins a new century of service, they can look back on some impressive achievements over the last one hundred years.

Who would have thought among the men in that 1922 vintage photograph that this organization would continue serving the community well into the next century?

It took hard work, strong friendships, and a little faith to make it all happen.

Century Cities

Big balloons are used to mark the City of Livingston's 100th anniversary. Photo: Steve Newvine

It's remarkable when a city can celebrate a special milestone such as a one-hundredth anniversary.

But when two cities less than ten miles apart can mark a centennial, it is nothing short of spectacular.

That was the case in two Merced County, California cities in 2022.

Atwater and Livingston in the Central Valley each celebrated this special milestone in a big way.

Atwater marked the passing of this special time in the City's history with a special timepiece. A large clock and tower was finished earlier in the year and dedicated over the summer.

The new centennial clock in downtown Atwater.
Photo: Steve Newvine

The clock was envisioned as a central point of focus for the City. In the months leading up to the dedication, the local government's City Hall was relocated to a refurbished space right across the street from the clock tower at 1150 5th Street.

The City had a special section on its webpage that includes a historical milestone listing and some black and white photos from several decades ago. The move to the new space permitted more space for staff and the many services now offered to residents as well as local businesses.

Several departments moved from space in the northern section of the city. The vacated space was repurposed for use by the City's Police Department.

This mural was painted at the Livingston Historical Museum in recognition of the City of Livingston's one-hundredth anniversary. Photo: Steve Newvine

Just a few miles north of Atwater, the City of Livingston is Merced County's other Centennial City in 2022.

The City formally marked the milestone on September eleventh; combining the one-hundredth anniversary celebration with a 9-11 invocation and moment of silence in honor of the victims of the 2001 terrorist attacks.

A centennial plaque near the entrance of the Livingston Historical Museum. Photo: Steve Newvine

Livingston's history includes having its own telephone company, a large concentration of Japanese immigrant families who were taken to internment camps during World War II, and a long-standing agricultural connection with sweet potatoes and grapes.

The cities of Atwater and Livingston are closely linked not only by the relatively short distance between the two but also by the agricultural heritage it shares.

Both are staying focused on the future as they continue to grow and contribute to the quality of life in Merced County.

Both are proud of their respective places along the back roads of California.

Medic Alert Pays it Forward

Medic Alert was founded as a non-profit organization in 1956 in Turlock, California.

This is a story about a teenager, her parents, and the start of a non-profit organization that has saved many lives over the past seven decades.

Thanks to the Collins family paying it forward, an estimated four million people have been touched in life-saving ways.

The story begins in Turlock, Stanislaus County, California. It was 1953 and thirteen year-old Linda Collins cut herself while playing with her cousins.

She was taken to the ER where the doctor followed standard procedure and administered a tetanus antitoxin.

Linda had an allergic reaction to the antitoxin and went into a coma. She nearly died. Had her parents been with her at the time, they could have told the doctor about the allergy.

Chrissie Collins and her husband Dr. Marion Collins shared the belief that medical information should be made available to emergency personnel. Dr. Collins came up with the idea of a custom-made bracelet with information engraved on it to help emergency personnel know more about a patient's allergies and conditions. They started MedicAlert from their Turlock home. Photo;MedicAlert.org

Escaping a potential tragedy wore on the minds of Linda's parents: Dr. Marion Collins and his wife Chrissie.

From that point forward, Chrissie attached a small note to her daughter's bracelet stating what the allergy was in case something like what Linda went through should ever happen again.

But Chrissie and Marion knew there had to be a better way for medical professionals to get that kind of information. Their concern went beyond their own family.

They wondered how to prevent something like this from happening in any family. Within three years, the Collins' formed a non-profit organization that we now know as *MedicAlert*.

It was all based in the family's hometown of Turlock.

According to the *MedicAlert* website, the first bracelet was custom made by a San Francisco jeweler who inscribed Linda's allergies (she was also allergic to aspirin and sulfa).

Upon entering college in 1956, classmates saw the bracelet and asked about having some made for others with similar needs. The *MedicAlert* Foundation was formed as the Collins' family believed strongly that providing vital medical communication was a public service.

The bracelets led to other items of jewelry and eventually to the establishment of a 24-hour hotline for medical professionals to access critical information about the conditions of *MedicAlert* members.

Dr. Marion Collins was proud of the creation of Medic Alert.

On the non-profit's website, he is quoted: "I believe I can save more lives with *MedicAlert* than I ever can with my scalpel."

Dr Collins passed in 1977. Chrissie remained in Turlock in the years following her husband's death.

Chrissie served on the *MedicAlert* board and was known to ask pointed questions about the non-profit's operations and the foundation's huge computer system. She passed in 2001.

Linda graduated from Stanford University with a degree in nursing. She married, had three children, and later divorced. Linda was a gifted golfer, winning amateur titles including the California Women's Golf Association Championship.

She turned professional and won the LPGA (Ladies Professional Golf Association) Senior Teaching Division National Championship. She died from breast cancer in 2004.

A sign was erected at one of the entrances to the City of Turlock showing all the active civic clubs, and proudly reminding visitors that the City was the home of Medic Alert. Photo: MedicAlert.org

There's a story in Chrissie Collins obituary about how the community of Turlock came together to get *Medic Alert* up and running in the late 1950s.

In 1960 after a story ran in This Week magazine, an insert in Sunday newspapers, the non-profit received one-hundred thousand orders for *MedicAlert* bracelets.

Chrissie was quoted at the time that the whole town of Turlock worked out of the family room of their home to sign up new members and ship bracelets.

From that humble start in the mid-1950s to now nearly seventy years later, *MedicAlert* has over four million members in fifty countries. Members pay $35 to join, and $15 in annual dues. Over the years, the organization has entered into strategic alliances to expand the reach of the system.

For profit companies, such as *Citizen Watch*, license products such as the *Citizen Eco Watch* with the *Medic Alert* logo.

Medic Alert demonstrated that a near tragic situation could be turned into something positive. The non-profit estimates that four-thousand lives are saved annually thanks to the bracelet and the phone system that provides information on members to emergency personnel.

In 1981 the Kiwanis Club of Turlock presented a stone marker that was placed in front of the non-profit's office on Colorado Avenue. On the marker, these words were inscribed:

> *Medic Alert Foundation International. Founded on March 26, 1956 in Turlock , California by Marion C. Collins, MD to provide a lifetime of emergency medical identification for all people.*
>
> *Presented by the Kiwanis Club of Greater Turlock, March 26, 1981.*

Medic-Alert moved from Turlock to an office in Salida, Stanislaus County, in 2015. Four years later, it moved back to an office downtown Turlock. A year later, COVID forced all employees to work from home.

Lost in all this shuffling of the office is the location of that stone marker. No one seems to know where it ended up, or whether it is even intact.

Today, a sign in front of the non-profit's former office space is the only visible reminder of the connection between *Medic-Alert* and the City of Turlock.

That original medical ID bracelet that Linda wore is now stored in the Smithsonian Institution.

It represents the story of a teenage girl and her parents who would not let a near tragedy go to waste. According to the non-profit website, over four million Medic Alert members may very well owe their lives to the thoughtfulness of the Collins family of Turlock way back in the 1950s.

The Collins' story of paying it forward has established a seventy year legacy that began in

Pedaling with the Police

Bicyclists are welcomed to the Pedaling with the Police event sponsored by the Merced Police Department. Photo: Steve Newvine

Many California communities tout their networks of bicycle paths.

It's not uncommon on a spring Saturday morning to see groups of bicyclists pedaling the trails along Bear Creek in Merced.

But on one particular Saturday in 2022, a group of cyclists had a special escort. Officers from the Merced Police Department provided the leadership and protection for participants in the *Pedaling with the Police* riding event.

The group met at the Merced Open Air Stage in Applegate Park, and then headed along the Bear Creek trail to Parsons Avenue and on to a rest stop at Rahilly Park.

About thirty bicyclists of all ages took part in the event. "This is something the Department's Bike Unit wanted to do to for the community," said Police Community Affairs Officer Emily Foster.

A pair of older cyclists liked the idea of a police escort along the Bear Creek trail. "This is good for all of us," one of the pair said.

Once at the other end of the first leg of the ride, the bicyclists had traveled three-and-one-third miles. It was time for a break.

"We think it's important for everyone to know that police officers do a lot more for the community that what is seen in some of the media," Lieutenant Foster said.

"We're here now to have a lot of fun with our citizens."
All that was required for this six-and-a-half mile bike ride was a safe set of wheels, the stamina to complete the ride, and a positive attitude.

"C'mon dad," one seven year old encouraged his father as the ride was underway.

Whether it was a son with his dad, a daughter with her mom, or a husband-and-wife pair, folks were taking advantage of perfect bicycling weather.

The returning cyclists had a good workout in the fresh air, a nice outing on a spring day, and hopefully a better understanding about the role police officers play in keeping everyone safe.

Underpass Art

Muralist Martin Figueroa works on an underpass painting.
Photo: Steve Newvine

Something interesting is emerging along the state highways in parts of California.

The state government provided grant money for cities to solicit local artists for the creation of murals on some of the walls at underpasses.

In the City of Merced in the Central Valley, over three-hundred, fifty thousand dollars was spent with the state allocation to create eight murals at each of the City's highway underpasses.

While some question whether public art should be a bigger priority at a time when public safety is a big concern, the impact of a project like this has been felt in this community of sixty-thousand residents.

For eight hours a day, Martin Figueroa is a supervisor for an industrial insulation company. But in his free time, he is an artist.

His paintings have adorned public areas of local businesses. But recently, his painting canvass was a concrete wall beneath highway 99 along Canal Street in Merced.

Martin earned the opportunity to paint a mural on that wall. He's one of eight artists awarded grant dollars to create murals on underpass walls up and down the highway 99 corridor that passes through the City of Merced.

"It was my first large scale mural done just by myself," he said of this early summer project.

Martin says a friend encouraged him to submit a proposal when the solicitation was announced in May. There were no parameters as to what he could propose, although the City of Merced and Caltrans had the final say before awarding the project to him.

His tools include several canisters of colorful spray paint, and some regular paint that comes in a can. When I caught up with near the end of his project, he was applying black paint to the figures of three individuals who appear at the bottom right of the mural.

"These are my kids," he said proudly. "I'm really doing this for them."

Martin enjoyed working on this new piece of public art in the City of Merced. He grew up in the City, rode bikes all over the many neighborhoods, and skated at the local parks.

He says he was not bothered by the many cars, walkers, and bicyclists who passed by him while he was working on the project.

Martin hopes this project will lead to more opportunities to work as an artist. Photo: Steve Newvine

The noise above from the 99 highway did not seem to bother him at all either.

"No worries," he shrugged when he was reminded of the hundreds of motor vehicles speeding along above him while he worked.

His only mild concern is how long his original artwork will last before graffiti rears a destructive force. "I hope it doesn't happen," he says. "But I'm sure it will."

His three kids, ages ten, nine, and six along with his wife are supportive of his art. They encourage him to keep pursuing his passion.

So far, only his youngest has expressed interest in art. Martin hopes that the youngster's interest will grow over the years.

Martin's mural is called "Chase Your Dreams", and is a galaxy of stars in the deep recesses of space.
Photo: Steve Newvine

Helping young people to pursue their passion is why he is dedicated to this particular project.

"I hope all of these murals inspire the youth and others around town," he said.

He titled his mural "Chase Your Dreams" and from the story behind what it took to take him to this showcase art project, the title seems to fit the artist.

Enjoying the moment right after my first hole-in-one.
Photo: Newvine Personal Collection

A flag-down view of the hole-in-one ball in the cup.
Photo: Newvine Personal Collection

++

Golf Course Aficionado

The Hole in One

If you like the game of golf, chances are you will spend some time on a California golf course. After thirty-five years playing the game, I finally made the shot of a lifetime

My first hole-in-one in October of 2021. It happened on the number nine hole at St. Stanislaus Golf Course in Modesto..

Using my nine iron, the swing was smooth, the ball sailed high and landed softly about six feet in front of the cup. At that point, the ball rolled to destiny.

It was an eighty-seven yard finish to a thirty-five year journey. After calling my wife, I headed into the clubhouse. Golf tradition dictates that the golfer who makes a hole-in-one buys drinks for everyone at the clubhouse.

In my case, it was nine o'clock in the morning, and only Charlie, the manager on duty was there.

After telling him what happened, Charlie congratulated me and offered a cup of coffee.

"Free coffee for every hole-in-one," he joked.

We talked for several minutes and he shared with me stories about the two times he got a hole-in-one right there on the St. Stanislaus course. I thanked him, and headed home.

Later in the day, my wife and I celebrated with dessert at a local coffee house. She's been sort of a golf widow in the months since my retirement when my golf outings intensified.

I shared my accomplishment with friends on social media, at the coffee shop, and with golfers in casual conversations.

They have offered their congratulations. Some have been telling me of their attempts at golf's greatest accomplishment.

My former golf buddie Mike, living in the east coast, told me that in his fifty-two years of playing the game, he has yet to land that special shot.

A non-golfer relative took a stab at our advancing years with the comment "With age comes perfection!" She added six exclamation points.

A friend from high school suggested I should buy a lottery ticket in hopes my lucky streak continues. (I did not buy a ticket.)

Another friend challenged me with a gentle hope that I might get a few more before retiring from the sport.

My wife's cousin shared that her deceased dad would be proud. I saw her dad swing a golf club, and I knew he was a gifted golfer. She's right. Bob would be proud.

Another cousin said he got a hole-in-one while stationed at Guantanamo Bay, Cuba in the military a few decades ago. He said it was a complete fluke as he had only played that one time in his whole life.

In a golf league one summer, I was a witness to that special golf moment.

It was nearly twenty years ago when our friend Les made a hole-in-one. It was an amazing thing to witness. It was like going through a ritual. Seeing what appeared to be the ball falling in from about one-hundred yards away, driving our golf cart up to the green, walking up to the cup, and seeing the ball sitting at the bottom.

I reached out to Les in the days following my lucky shot. I shared my news and established a common bond that ties golfers together.

One last look at the hole where it happened. The mark on the green where the ball landed before rolling into the cup was repaired by me shortly after this shot was taken. Photo: Newvine Personal Collection

Good luck stayed with me on the golf course in the weeks and months following that fortunate October morning. Nine months later, on Independence Day, it happened again. It was on the same hole, using the same club.

The hole-in-one club has accepted me, and now I'm a lifetime member.

Stepping Up for a Friend

Dennis Gillen lived in Merced, California. He passed away in February 2022. Dennis gave me this 2018 photo he had another golfer snap for him at an area golf course.

You get to know someone real well when you have coffee with him every week. That was the case with my first California friend Dennis.

Golf connected me with Dennis. We were introduced at an informal golf league started by a local bank.

Every Wednesday night in the summer of 2006, Dennis and I joined several other golfers to play the game and build relationships.

The golf group folded when the bank folded. Most of the golfers went their separate ways, but Dennis and I remained connected.

Dennis and I would continue our connection by driving on the back roads of California to a beautiful course called Stevinson Ranch.

We played one of the final rounds ever at Stevinson Ranch before it closed in 2015. With me taking a vacation day from work, we said farewell to one of the finest golf courses either of us had the pleasure of playing. Shortly after that day, the owners closed up shop and converted the property to agricultural land.

Golf connected me with Dennis and we enjoyed one of the final rounds at the former Stevinson Ranch course in Merced County. Photo: Newvine Personal Collection.

We played golf dozens of times during the years after I moved to Merced. We had weekly coffee breaks for about ten years straight. Like I said, you get to know someone well when you have coffee with him every week.

When a friend passes, we remember the good times, the pearls of wisdom, and even the challenging moments.

Thinking back on the life of my friend Dennis, there were plenty of items in each category. He passed at age eighty-three.

With regard to wisdom, Dennis offered life experiences. He lost his mom tragically when he was just five years old. His marriage that produced three children ended in divorce.

As I brought up issues I was dealing with at work, he would share lessons learned from customers during his forty-plus years in his working career.

All of this and more was shared between friends whether on the golf course or at our weekly coffee breaks at a local cafe.

The challenges in this friend-to-friend relationship came in the final years of his life. As his health declined I became aware of just what friendship is all about.

At this stage of our decade-and-a-half friendship, I realized I would be carrying more of the investment in time and energy to help my friend. When he couldn't drive, I (and other friends) would help him get to church, to a store, or to his credit union.

Our weekly coffee breaks continued at his home as I brought in the beverages and visited him for a couple of hours each week. Every time I talked to him, he'd end the conversation with the words "God bless."

I'm grateful that in what became the final months of his life, Dennis never let me forget how much he appreciated our bond. Rarely did one of those weekly coffee breaks end without Dennis telling me how thankful he was that I was his best friend.

I needed to hear that.

So when a friend passes, we recall the good times. We extract tidbits of conversation that stick with us forever. We make sense out of the challenging moments. And we realize that it is in these darker times when real friends are called upon to step up. It's what friends do for each other.

He Has Seen a Lot of Back Roads

*Charlie packing golf tees for sale at the golf pro shop.
Photo: Steve Newvine*

If there is anyone who knows something about the back roads of California, it is probably Charlie. He's a ninety-year old who spent most of his life in Modesto, Stanislaus County.

His family moved to the state on a back road in 1934 when he was just six months old. His family was part of the Dust Bowl exodus that brought so many families from the middle of the country to California during the Great Depression.

"We came from Arkansas," Charlie said. "My parents, siblings, and even the family German Shepard made the trip here."

Taking the dog on the eighteen-hundred mile trip may seem ordinary, until Charlie explains where the dog had to stay in order to make the journey.

"The dog would lay between the car bumper and the radiator," he says with a smile. "There was enough space for him. There was no room in the car as it was packed with all our belongings."

In California, Charlie became quite familiar with the back roads in the Central Valley region growing up. While there were cars along those dirt roads and valley lanes back in his youth, he traversed along the roadways on his horse. That was what transportation was like in the rural California during the 1940s.

"We thought nothing of it," he said. "All the farmers around here had horses."

Most of the farmers had tractors and cars too. Charlie was behind the wheel of a tractor before going into first grade. By age eight, he would drive the family car on errands near the family homestead. He did not have a license, but he could drive.

"One time, when I was in seventh grade, I was falling behind in one of my subjects," he shared over coffee in the golf course pro shop where he works part time. "My teacher told me she'd help me if I could come by her house after supper. I told my dad about it, and he told me to take the car."

It was during that trip that he was pulled over by a law enforcement officer. The officer asked Charlie how old he was and where he was heading. After Charlie told him, the officer said, "Well, I've been tracking you for the past few miles, and you're doing all right, so go on, and be careful."

As a young man in the 1950s and 1960s, Charlie watched as the vast patches of rural farmland started the conversion to industrial and commercial use. From the counter at the golf course pro shop, he points out several parcels where shopping centers and warehouses now stand, and recalls the time when the land was used to grow fruits and vegetables.

The same holds true for Modesto, where Charlie worked at a

dairy processing plant. "That particular plant was laid out over a couple of City blocks," he said. "It's all gone today."

He owned and operated a fast food and soft ice cream shop for a number of years. When he sold the business, he went to work for a hardware store. "I would go in to that store two or three times a week to find something for a project I'd be working on," he said.

One day, the owner asked him if he would work for the store. "I told him on one condition, I need to have Sunday off. The owner said, 'You want Sundays off so you can go to church?' I told him no, Sundays off because I have a standing tee time for golf with my friend."

A lot has changed.

Charlie and his wife raised a family from a home they share on one of these former back roads. He's worked a variety of jobs primarily centered on agriculture.

Without really putting a finger on the key to his success at work, anyone talking to him can tell you his secret is a strong work ethic. He's on the job before the golf course officially opens, and he keeps himself busy with pro shop duties when not checking in golfers who will play the course on any summer day. He knows his customers well and can be relied upon by his boss and his coworkers.

He works at the golf course five days a week, saying that remaining active keeps him sharp.

The key to his longevity centers on his favorite outdoor activity: golf.

When he's not working at the golf course, he spends his days off on difference courses playing the game with his friends.

"Working keeps me active, golf keeps me going."

++

Memory Movers

Where Were You in 1973?- Stimulating Memories from Fifty Years Ago

If you're over fifty, reminisce along with me. If you're under fifty, read this anyway because your day is coming.

Community museums keep local history alive with their permanent collections of photographs and icons from years gone by.

Some, like the Merced Courthouse Museum, will do special exhibits centering of a specific aspect of a community's history.

In 2023, the Museum staged an exhibit that focuses on the year 1973.

Using photographs acquired from the *Merced Sun Star* newspaper and other sources, the rooms of the Museum were alive with memories from that particular time fifty years ago.

The photos included the successful completion of an important bridge project, protests over a plan to build the County office building in front of the Courthouse, and other events from that year. Even how the community dealt with the Arab Oil Embargo got a photographic representation in the exhibit.

As the year began, gas was thirty-nine cents a gallon. By October, the price would go up and rationing would start thanks to the Embargo. The higher prices for gas likely restricted a lot of recreational travel along the back roads of California.

This ARCO station attendant stands next to a gasoline pump in 1973 Merced. The sign reads "Rationing Today". Gas rationing started shortly after the Arab Oil Embargo began. Photo: Merced Courthouse Museum

The exhibit included icons from 1973 within the display cases. Vinyl record albums, a fondue set, and a sample of the fashions worn by the hip wannabees of the era were included.

Plaid pants for the guys and a polka-dot skirt for the ladies were displayed on two mannequins.

Among the photos was a series of three shots of the dissembling of a shopping center sign from downtown Merced in the winding down days of urban renewal.

Display cases show icons from 1973. In the background of this photo is a sampling of fashion choices from that time. There is no truth to reports that I loaned the museum a pair of my seventies' plaid pants for this exhibit. Photo: Steve Newvine

But for many of us, especially those who did not live in California in 1973, the exhibit afforded an opportunity to look back on our lives fifty years ago.

I was a sixteen year old who just got a driver permit. Walking out of the Department of Motor Vehicles

Department, then housed inside the Lewis County (New York) Courthouse building, my dad said to me, "Now you'll have to learn how to drive."

I ran my first red light within minutes as I was leaving the village of Lowville. That was not a great start. But somehow, I got better at obeying the rules of the road.

Steve as a teen. I'm in the top row center of this photo of the South Lewis High School Tennis Club from 1973. Photo: The Talon (South Lewis High School Yearbook)

On weekday mornings in my hometown back in 1973, the sounds of two announcers at radio station WBRV would help me get moving for the day.

George and Ed hosted a popular morning show with segments that served as signals for me to get myself in gear to make it to the school bus stop near my house.

Here was the routine: breakfast by the 7:00 AM news, brush teeth by the 7:20 *Swap Shop* program, homework papers and school books ready to go by the 7:30 weather report, and out the door to the bus stop by the 7:40 sports program.

The bus arrived shortly before 8:00 and I was on my way to high school.

Steve's parents. My mom and dad from about fifty years ago. Photo: Newvine Personal Collection

In 1973, my family was among the fortunate to have cable TV. Gone were the days of using an antenna to capture two or three stations within range of the stations' transmitting towers.

In 1973 with cable TV, we now had an amazing ten channels from which to choose.

One of those stations was WPIX in New York City where my brother could watch practically every Yankee game, and where my dad and I could watch reruns of *The*

Honeymooners. I can proudly say that I knew the dialogue of each episode of the original thirty-nine episodes before I entered college.

Ralph and Ed from the *Honeymooners* were almost as common as the daily drop-in visits from my Grandma and Grandpa Newvine, my great aunt Myrtle, our neighbor Fred and others who always found Bea and Stub's home warm and welcoming.

Instant coffee with some kind of baked good was always served to our nightly visitors. If there was time, a game of cards would keep us entertained.

1973 was a special year for the community of Merced in California. It was a time that made an impression on all of us, even if you did not live here.

But looking back, if you were around back in 1973, take a moment or two to recall the music, the hairstyles, and even the attitudes.

In many ways, not much has changed.

++

Wrapping it Up

These back roads have taken us all over California, and in some cases, into the back roads of our collective memory.

We've been to the coast, to the mountains, and to the regions north and south of the palm and the pine.

The people have opened up their hearts as they share their stories and a small part of their lives.

We know we can't stay forever, and we're thankful to have spent what time we had going back to life along the back roads of California.

There are more memories to share, more cups of coffee to pour, more selfies to snap on our phones and more places to experience.

California gets a bad rap at times. The taxes are too high. The prices are too expensive. The traffic can be a bear. Name a problem, and California probably has a story to top it.

But California has great weather most of the time. California people can be among the nicest folks you'll ever meet. You can travel from ocean view to mountain vistas in just a few hours.

You can drink some of the finest wine in the world. You may experience avocado on a regular basis. You might even want to try an order of garlic fries. It's all here.

There's bad, there's good, and there's California. Enjoy it from afar when you see a news story about the latest issue impacting the west. Experience it close up from a guided tour in Hollywood or San Francisco. Or take it all in from the front seat of a car travelling along the back roads.

If there's one thing I've learned from life in California it's to take the back roads whenever possible. Literally, back roads have saved me frustration from highway traffic jams. Symbolically, the back roads mean more than an alternative route to a destination. By slowing down, I've opened myself up to meet interesting people and experience a more genuine California.

Stay on the back roads. You will like the view from there.

Acknowledgements

As a number of the chapters here started as columns on MercedCountyEvents.com , I wish to thank webmaster Brad Haven for providing my regular writing home for now going on nearly a decade-and-a-half.

I'd also like to thank three English teachers who indirectly share some responsibility for helping me become a writer

Mrs. Gaylord and Mrs. Burdick were my English teachers in junior high. While they never uttered the words "you should be a writer" to me, both had a respect for grammar, spelling, and structure that stuck with me over the years.

Then there was Mr. Gehrlein who was my senior high school English teacher. I'd like to say we had some special bond with him, but even he, rest his soul, would agree that was not the case. What he did do was allow our class to experiment with many forms of expression. He once assigned a term paper on rock music, allowing us to pick a musician and tell their story. I chose Elvis Presley.

He let the entire class experiment with newly acquired video equipment. We produced a version of *The Match Game*. I was the host.

I had a good mix of English structure and outside-the-box learning in high school. Those three teachers have my gratitude.

Recipe

Eggplant Parmesan

1 medium eggplant

½ pound mozzarella

4 small cans tomato sauce

½ cup parmesan cheese

1 teaspoon oregano

1 ½ cups breadcrumbs

2 eggs

Pinch of salt

Peel and slice eggplant. Dip in egg and breadcrumbs. Fry to a golden brown on both sides. Layer in a 13" x9" pan: eggplant, mozzarella cheese, 2 cans tomato sauce, 1 teaspoon oregano, parmesan cheese. Repeat with the remainder of these ingredients. Bake for 30 minutes at 350 degrees.

(From the Lake Erie Girl Scout Council 1984 Cookbook)

About the author

Steve Newvine became a television journalist and worked on camera and behind the scenes for eleven years. He was a reporter, anchor, Executive Producer, Special Projects Manager and News Director at five television stations.

In that career, he did a variety of things. Be he gravitated to writing and producing documentaries that required a great deal of storytelling.

Transitioning into the world of running chambers of commerce, Steve wrote travel brochures, public policy statements and monthly newsletters for thirteen years. It was storytelling intended to motivate business owners, local government leaders and families considering where to spend their vacations.

When he left that world behind to work for a public utility, Steve couldn't seem to put the keyboard down. For thirteen years, he wrote a monthly news update for the participants in the utility programs he managed. His goal was to keep everyone in the loop.

Steve has written about a dozen books over the past fifteen years. His columns on MercedCountyEvents.com continues now in its fourteenth year.

He enjoys running, collecting recorded music and playing golf. He and his wife will celebrate their 44th anniversary in 2024. They have two grown daughters and one grandchild.

Made in United States
Orlando, FL
24 October 2025